No More Mistakes
Guide to Making Better Decisions

DeShawn Kenner

ISBN: 0989785408
ISBN-13: 978-0989785402

Layout by Sarah Anne Hubbard

Kenner Publishing
Lindenhurst, New York

Printed in the U.S.A.

DEDICATION

To Anyone who has ever made a mistake.

CONTENTS

"A smart man learns from his own mistakes…but a wise man learns from the mistakes of others"

~Old Ancient Proverb

DeShawn Kenner

Introduction

They say insanity is doing the same thing over and over again, expecting different results. Yet many of us still cling onto the same old patterns and habits (the bad ones of course) and expect things to change for the better. However, nothing changes in fact 99% of the time things get worse when we stay on that particular road: which leads to failure, depression, or even death.

For instance, how many smokers wait until they start to cough up blood due to their lungs being so abused and polluted, that they can no longer take the pain of their own habit? This forces them to finally stop, or go to the doctor only to be diagnosed with cancer or some other related health issue, and some don't even stop then! They do not see the consequences until something is removed before they are made believers. Overall, why take it that far? Why subject yourself to unnecessary pain and suffering? Why be selfish and only think of yourself, especially if you have a family that loves and depends on you? Friends who could not imagine if you are not around for the laughs, good times, bad times, or just to be there when they need a shoulder to lean on.

The saying goes "birds of a feather flock together" if that is the case, then the whole crew needs this book. Even still, everybody is their own unique person with the ability to choose which way they walk, talk, or live. I know a lot of us grew up hearing things from our family like "you act just like your father" or "you are just like your mother" etc... Although, in our young infancy and adolescent years of life we may mimic the people and attitudes that surround us, which does not negate the fact that we are always at liberty to do what suits us best. How many kids pick out their own clothes on a daily basis to wear to school based on what they think is cool or matches? The point is from a young age we start making our own choices even if only on a small scale based on what we like, want, need, and are in our own personal best interest. When you think about it from this perspective, there should be no reason to make the same errors continuously. How many of us after being foolish enough to play with fire as youngsters, without supervision or proper instruction, felt the rude awakening of pain from a burn? I can just about guarantee that anyone with this experience never mishandled fire again and treated it with care and respect.

Now I know that there is a "special group of people" who would challenge the thought or example I just laid down, they may say something like "just because you got burned by the flame doesn't mean you stop using it," on the contrary that should make you want to learn how to use fire safely, then master it. I agree to a point, in the sense that just because you failed at something once doesn't mean you shouldn't try again to succeed at it or even excel past that goal. Just as President Barack Obama failed to get elected in his run for The House of Representatives, however went on to become a Senator and then President of the United States of America. Both of these appointments are viewed as more revered positions and some would even say more powerful. Moreover, in the context that I am writing there are some failures that should not ever be repeated. Let's say one person murders another person for whatever reason, then gets caught, convicted, and sentenced. Upon release should this person convicted think, "Alright, I got caught for the first murder, but how can I get away with the next one?" No, of course! Some would say this is a moral issue, but my point is why someone is even thinking about killing again. The example may have been a little dramatic, but I needed to be clear on how far a bad decision can go. All ideas and thoughts sprout from the mind. So I would say that example is for a person convicted of that crime or any other crime. One should plan on living right and doing the right thing upon release, scratch the whole thought of how you could get over if you did it again, or even the thought that you would do it again. Just thinking about it with that state of mind is a bad idea. We will return to this topic a little later on in the book.

We will explore a range of options for the different situations that one may find themselves in; how to stop blaming our poor choices on other people, take responsibility, and be in control of our own lives through sound logical decisions (in some cases they do not even require logic). If you were standing on top of the roof of a one hundred story building and the person you admired the most asked you to jump off the side and it was perfectly safe, how many of you would fulfill that request? Ask a few of the dumbest people you know this question and compare their responses to those of a few of the smartest people you know. I doubt regardless of their IQ gaps, that their answers would be drastically different.

You've already made a great choice just by picking up this book. You've started on the journey to making your life an easy and happy one to live. Enjoy this read, think critically, logically, rationally, and keep an open mind. Remember "each one, teach one," or two if you can!

Jewel 1: Being Spontaneous, Impulsive

When a relationship starts between two new lovers, there is an exciting new energy. There is a romance so to speak, where everything is still mysterious. Maybe one lover out of the blue shows up two o'clock in the morning with roses in a limo, and a private jet waiting to fly the two of you off to an exotic retreat somewhere in the Caribbean, without a care for their day to day obligations. Now unless one of the two is super rich and never has to work a day in his or her life, and can promise you the same lifestyle forever, I would not recommend getting on that plane or for that matter even leaving your home. It has been said that a promise is a comfort to a fool, so I would want that promise written into a legal contract and signed.

Think of all the spur of the moment lust filled sexual encounters, which have created countless unplanned children. If these unwanted children were even born, because some are left at the abortion clinics across the world to be disposed of in whatever manner the doctor chooses. This is not a discussion regarding whether abortion is right or wrong, or the use of condoms and safe sex never ending argument. However it is highlighting impulsive decisions that lead up to unwanted consequences. Say you were out drinking, smoking weed, popping ecstasy, and whatever else may be used to cloud one's inhibitions and thoughts; those factors should not be used as an excuse for being reckless. I have drank hard liquor and smoked some of the most powerful hydro on earth, and these influences didn't make me do anything I would not have done anyway, but that is just me. I still knew not to violate a woman no matter how intoxicated I became, to respect her personal space and not over do it. I played the dog and cat games but I never lost sight of the lines not to cross.

Nor would I have walked out into highway

traffic or used my high as an excuse to go on a murderous spree. I think the vast majority of people who have ever gotten high, do it and fall back or just do what they normally do. Besides the adverse effects substances have on balance, reflex responses, and personal deterioration of an individual's own health. Speaking from personal experience, overall one is still aware of the things around them; maybe not the most on point but aware nonetheless. That is why it is against the law to drink and drive, not because you are not conscious, but your reflex response and focus is not ice pick sharp.

There are times when we have to make split second decisions. For example to stand in the way of a speeding car or move out of the way as fast as you can, or to save a person who has fallen into a body of water, that will drown if not helped. In situations like these it is understandable to react rapidly, because a life at that moment depends on it. In everyday life, decisions are not that demanding, there is always a little extra time to think and a few more options to consider. One of the biggest mistakes today is living every day as it is your last. This cliché's saying is in my opinion wrong. Although, any day could be our last on earth, it is still the wrong ideology. I will explain the indirect psychological message is that there may be no tomorrow; so live recklessly and haphazardly today. Now you and I may understand the cliché as tell everybody how you feel, do everything you desire, eat all you want, etc..., but realistically should that be done? Should you walk into your workplace on one of those days that you are living like your last and blank out on your supervisor because you don't like them? Now maybe if you have another job already lined up that could work for you, but with times being so hard economically a job is considered an asset just like a home or car. Things such as these mean it would not be beneficial to keep your emotions on display. I find it better to take a look at any situation at least twice, as the carpenter's saying goes, "check twice and cut once," so always think twice.

The words to live by should be, "live everyday like there is a tomorrow." Who thinks about dying every day? Who isn't looking forward to the future, towards a brighter day? Who doesn't want to see the kids grow up or see that someone special? WHO? There is always something to look forward to, with that in mind do not rush anything. Most times being spontaneous means that you are over anxious about something, a "panic" sets in, and if you don't do it right now you will never have the opportunity to do it again. The person being impulsive, will cut corners from anything to snatch up the so called once in a lifetime opportunity, like not using protection to overdoing it in any arena of life. Cutting corners only makes a circle in which you will only keep going around and around. Have patience, you do not put rice into the pot before the water starts to boil, nor do you harvest a crop before the right season.

Jewel 2: Not Seeing the Future

I think not seeing the future is worse than being spontaneously impulsive. What is not seeing the future? Simply put, it is failing to strategically plan for the future. It is the not knowing what you want, where you want to be, what you want to be, what type of life you want to live, how you want to look, what type of people you want to be around, and most importantly how you will obtain all these things.

The civilized world is already on track all one must do is get on the right train to where they want to go. A demonstration of this is going to school, after the first grade one goes to the second, third, fourth, fifth, sixth, and so on. This is already planned out, all one has to do is be there and do what needs to be done. Imagine after first grade no one had any idea on what to do next, where would all the first graders go?

Luckily that has already been planned out long before the first grade ever arrived.

At some point in life we become responsible for making our own plans, especially if we do not like the blueprint someone else has laid out for us. If you do not like the plan someone else has laid out for you and you don't have one of your own, then you are going to be in a lot of trouble! In some cases being an actor or actress on someone else's show may mean a short acting career, so why not write your own script and make yourself the star?

Going back to the first jewel, as I said in so many words is everything takes time, so do not try to squeeze everything into one day or even one week, month, or year. Trying to reach your goals through your strategic plans in one day especially the big goals: owning your own business, losing a lot of weight, buying a home, earning a master's or doctorate, or even getting married will not happen overnight. If you can visualize your plans into reality and know that they will happen, than you will succeed. At the very least you will spend every living day of your life like it is your last doing what you planned for yourself. Planning ahead and visualizing the end that you have in mind for yourself, also relieves a great deal of stress and anxiety because you know what has to be done. Everything is always easier when you know what needs to be done. Needless to say, we always have to be ready to readjust our plans, but even that is easy, if you expect things to change, especially the things that you cannot change.

When making your plans, know what you want. If you started working out and wanted stronger more defined abdominal muscles you would not work on your shoulders, nor if you wanted a stronger chest would you be doing squats. For stomach you would be doing sit ups and for chest you would be doing bench presses. The key is to have a clear picture in your mind of what mission you want to complete and bring to reality. By not working on the specific thing you need to complete your goal, you are wasting valuable time out of your life.

Know what you want and go for it! If you went out to eat and had your mind set on getting some chicken because it had been on your mind all day, and when you finally order your meal you ask for a cheeseburger and fries instead of chicken, who would be to blame for that? Whose fault would it truly be? I will answer that for you…YOURS! Especially since you knew what you wanted and didn't go for it, in fact you went and worked against yourself. You knocked your own self out cold. This is the case with most of us today, we work against ourselves, and we are our own worst enemy. The failure to plan or the planning in case of failure is attributed to a few factors, one of them being discipline, the subject of our next jewel.

Jewel 3: Discipline

The word and meaning of discipline have a bad name, the typical person when thinking of this term or asked what it means, the first thing that comes to mind is punishment or oppression. When in reality what discipline is designed to do is bring order to a situation or one's own life. Without order there can only be disorder. Disorder brings about chaos which in turn brings about a breakdown of a structure and certain destruction follows.

Imagine the world we live in without any rules, no order, and no discipline. Do you think the world would be safe for you and your family? No it would not be, especially if law and order were not enforced. In the context that I'm presenting this to you, you have to be disciplined and get yourself in order or you will destroy yourself, because you will not be safe from you.

Every person is their own world and metaphorically speaking if the person does not take care of their own world it will become polluted, toxic, and hazardous to everything around it, but most of all to its self. Nobody wants to be around anything that is polluted and filled with toxic waste. Would you want to spend your days and nights hanging out with a drunk, drug addicted, filthy street bum?

Authority as well, is not a bad thing. If you hate authority, you can never be an authoritative figure. Which means you will always be told what to do because you despise giving orders or telling anybody what to do, even your own self. That is the old rebel attitude; however the rebel is never really in control of their own self or in a situation that they are involved in. They are disruptive at most and live confused, uncertain, and unstable lives. Realistically, most rebels are so because they want order. Think about all the rebellious protests you can think of. Like the rebellious Dr. Martin Luther King Jr. who organized boycotts and marches in essence for order or The Hippies of the Sixties, who had their protest to end a war. The Boston Tea Party this rebellion was to bring order, get justice with taxes, and ultimately freedom. Nobody likes abusive authority, such as the England Monarchy during the 1700s. I think that plays a major role in why most people hate to be governed or to govern. Whether they come from an abusive home, state, or country is more likely why a person could be turned off to rule.

We cannot hate discipline, order, or authority so much that we cannot even control our own selves, because like with anything else an internal rebellion will arise. If we cannot control our eating habits, then its starts to show with excess fat. If gaining weight is not enough to take control of our own selves by making prominent decisions with our out of control indulgence, then things like high blood pressure, diabetes, and heart disease join in on the riot and rally against your out of control style, in hopes that you would govern yourself in a more just manner.

If you love your life, you will embrace authority, discipline, and order wholeheartedly. A life without them can only be filled with anxiety, chaos, and confusion. Where you will always be told what to do because you neglect to realize what must be done. Take control of your life though...

Jewel 4: Responsibility

Remember when you got that 100% on a test, got that guy or girl you were after, or made that money that was yours? That was all of your own doing. Your studying got you that 100% on that test, the way you presented yourself got you the hook up with that guy or girl, and your hard work or know how made you the money you earned. So you take full credit for those achievements and why shouldn't you, you did that.

So here is what I advise you do, just like you have taken credit for all your successes, take credit for all your failures and screw ups. It is only right to do so. Do not ever get caught up in the blame game, one should not accept the good times and not the bad times or the yeses and not the no's, take the bitter with the sweet. For the thug and thugette who blames their misfortunes on society would he or she credit their fortunes to society? Attribute their pot of gold, platinum, and diamonds to their own hustle and ambitions to overcome? Of course you would want credit for your own good work; you would probably give a shout out to those who have helped you accomplish your goal. Overall, it was and is all you. We are in a time when average just won't do. A GED will hardly get you a job at McDonald's. It is your responsibility to overachieve and go from ordinary to extraordinary!

How do you do that? First, blame no one else for your short comings. Second, wholeheartedly accept all of the challenges that life will offer you, face them head on. In martial arts like kung fu and jujitsu, you can't get a black belt until you face all of your competitors, in some cases four and five will attack you at a time. You must be ready, willing, and able to not only face but also defeat all these challenges at the same time. You don't get a black belt for beating up a baby, nor do you have sharp eye sight because you can see an elephant that is right in front of you in broad daylight. Nor do you have great hearing because you can hear loud music in the same room that you are in. Earn your mental black belt in responsibility by embracing adversity and multitasking with constant practice. Hard work is said to be better than talent alone, I know and believe this is true. The people who are usually the most responsible, feel the most empowered. Free yourself by taking matters into your own hands, as long as they are beneficial in upgrading yourself, those around you, and the world if possible. You are required to think ahead and for others at times, that is your responsibility.

Jewel 5: Good Quality is Everything

Keep in mind when you are doing anything from eating to doing business, quality is everything. Basically, in a short definition, good quality is when something is or done to the best it can be. It's the difference between the student who gets an 'A' in class from the student who gets the 'C' in the same class. In the long run the student who gets the best grades will hear from the better schools when it is time to graduate high school. The person, who eats healthier, choosing fruits and vegetables over cookies and potato chips, or any junk food, can expect to feel and look healthier. Those who choose water and milk over soda and liquor can expect better results on their health as well, provided you are not allergic to them.

These are all just small examples of the bigger picture. It's very important you study, plan, and know exactly what it is you are doing. If you were going to the barber shop or the beauty salon, would you want to sit in the chair of the barber or hairstylist who took their time and knew what they were doing and gives you the best hair style possible? Would you sit in the chair of the barber or hairstylist who did not know what they were doing, rushing or not? Of course you would hop in the chair of the person who is going to do it right with quality work, I would. So if you do something, then do it right. If you do the best business possible in whatever business you do, people will keep coming back to do business with you. If you do right by your mind and body, they will do right by you. If you sleep good, exercise good, and take good care of your health then you will look good and live longer.

If you think good thoughts and read things that will help you grow stronger mentally, you will grow to be a more intelligent critical thinker. Reading all things will help you grow and improve the quality of your mind. That extends into love as well, in order to be the best lover you would have to apply what you know. The same is true for a poor quality warrior or fighter. A fighter who does not train their body and mind, and does not practice their fighting techniques regularly will surely get beat or killed by the fighter who does. Whatever you do, do it to the best of your ability or don't do it at all. Good quality skill is the point that separates success from failure. I would rather own one beautiful mansion than to own ten run down shacks. I would rather have one healthy mate then ten sick mates. I would rather have one car that works well instead of ten that don't even run.

Quality over quantity, always seek to better your quality of life through your mind, body, spirit, and actions.

Jewel 6: Being the Know-it-All

It is said that the person who really knows something knows that they really know nothing at all. However, there are those people who know nothing, but think they know everything. The bottom line is this, if you don't know something just say you don't know! Don't waste your time or anyone else's with stupid unnecessary mistakes, errors, or with wrong guesses. It could cost somebody money or physical harm to someone, and make you look like a liar.

Being a know-it-all allows no room to know or learn anything else; knowledge is infinite and never ending. There is always something more to know and learn. Always give yourself mental space for growth and development; because opinions, ideas, theories, and even facts can change. More than five hundred years ago, even a little more current than that it was considered a fact that the world was flat, or that horses and cheetahs were the fastest moving things on the planet, which cars and airplanes have changed. What will replace them? Can they be replaced? Keep your mind open, nobody knows what is next.

Those who believe they know it all, never learned one of the most vital skills, how to listen. You cannot give an accurate answer if you never hear and listen to the question. I also believe that you cannot fully understand and know yourself if you won't, don't, and refuse to listen to your own self.

There is a lot you can learn from you, about your own self if you would just hear yourself out. Just be quiet and listen to your number one fan and listener, yourself. You will be surprised at what you have to say and will learn and find out something you did not know.

Jewel 7: Learn, Understand, and Use the Power of Words to Communicate Effectively

Every year millions of people get into violent physical fights, for one specific reason, they don't know how to talk. Never underestimate the power of words, they mean something. The words of a person can build, heal, kill, soothe, relax, scare, and help among many other things such as sexually stimulate or turn a person off.

Be careful what you say and who you say it around, you never know who is listening. People listen when you least expect them to be, even when they act like they are not listening. If someone told or asked you to look to your left, you would look to your left and vice verse with your right. It would be something if someone told you to watch your step because you were about to step on a nail. You would look to see if the nail was there, this is because words mean something, they have great power. They can make you laugh or cry, love or hate, so watch what you say, choose your words carefully.

A great part of President Obama's success stems from the way he speaks; he understands the value of words. The old saying "sticks and stones may break my bones, but words will never hurt me," needs to be revised. Words can most certainly hurt you; they can break your heart. It is not what you say, but how you say it. Learn how to talk the talk well.

Jewel 8: Talk is Cheap

A great word play is strong and necessary in the game of life, however actions will reign supreme. Somebody telling you that they are going to punch you in the face does not hold the same weight as someone who actually punches you in the face. You can talk about what you are going to do, but it is not real until you actually perform the act. Words just describe or can tell somebody what you are going to do, but if you don't do what you say; your words will lose value, if you don't have a valid excuse for not doing what you said you would. I could talk someone's head off about writing a book but it wouldn't happen unless I put pen to paper, like Nike says, "Just Do It!"

Similar to Jewel 4, this jewel represents fulfilling your obligations. Those who live it rarely have to talk it. Most of those who talk it don't really live it, unless you just the outright flashy type. For me, these two jewels symbolize not only just taking care of myself, but also my family and community. First, start with yourself, because if you can't care for yourself it is unlikely you can care for anyone else as with family, community, or even a pet. I am not just talking about taking care of you financially. I'm talking about all aspects of you: body, mind, health, and soul. Make a choice to be around people who bring you peace and joy. Remember, if you hang with dirty dogs sooner or later you are coming up with fleas. A person does not win a race by just dreaming about it, the person has to actually run it. You must train yourself to do what you say you are going to do.

You can start with something as simple as promising yourself a glass of water a day, by drinking that glass of water you have fulfilled an obligation to yourself. Keep your own word, start small, and work your way up.

Jewel 9: Man Up...Stand on Your Own Two Feet

There are times when we all need help, nobody can deny that. However, when you are able to do it for yourself, then do so. Don't sit around waiting for a handout like somebody owes you something, because unless you worked for a paycheck or won on the horse that you bet on down at the track, nobody owes you anything! So the sooner you get that in your head, the better. That means brush your teeth and wash your own ass, because if you don't you will be the one with the bad breath and a stinking behind. Male or female learn to cook for yourself, wash your own clothes, brush your own hair, braid it, and style it, whatever.

Fellas learn how to shape your own self up, practice good grooming habits all away around the board. About the welfare thing, if you're in a jam and need to get on your feet real quick and have no other option, then use it but don't abuse it. Don't make a career of living off a handout, if you are physically and mentally capable to make your own moves do it. If there is nothing out there you like, create something you like to do and turn it into a business. If you want to be the boss, think like the boss and not just a worker. Think about how to create jobs and create money, and then make it happen. Until then stay focused and stack your money the old fashion way, by earning it. I don't care if you have to shovel crap or pick cotton, these aren't the slavery days and nobody is forced to do anything, but the paper chase is the paper chase. Get it how you live and don't cry about it. Like the Bible says, "God helps those who help themselves."

Jewel 10: Education

Information is everywhere so take advantage of it, the more you know the better you will live. There are a ton of curriculums to learn from. Life itself being the biggest education, with all the knowledge, wisdom, understanding, and experience you can get just by living day to day. It is not enough to just live, you have to live consciously and be aware of what is going on around you. There is a lot to learn about you, which is an adventure of discovery on its own. I recommend you take time just to get to know yourself. How does one accomplish this? First you have to be willing to be brutally honest with yourself about you. Then you can start off with the known facts about yourself, name, birthday, mother's & father's names, height, weight, favorite food, etc…Then ask yourself something a bit more challenging, like are you a success or are you becoming a failure, why are you failing in your situation, and what can you do to start winning?

When learning yourself just like anything else you are figuring out, start out with these words: who, what, when, where, why, and how? Who am I? What do I want out of life? When will I stop wasting my time? Where do I see myself ten years from now? Why have I been wasting time? How do I start to get myself together? These are just a few examples on how to use these words. You can remix the questions however you like, don't be afraid to ask yourself the tough questions about you. Don't be afraid to respond, nor deny it, nor be apprehensive when asking yourself why you feel the way you feel about the questions you may ask yourself. I know the rumor that says if you talk to yourself, you are crazy, but I believe differently. If you can't talk to yourself, then you can't talk to anybody else. It's the same dynamic as helping yourself; if you can't help yourself then you can't help anyone else. That's how songs are written, math problems solved, and overall civilization is built and enhanced. Thinking things out, this means not only that you have to talk to yourself, but have to answer yourself. Knowing yourself is of utmost importance, not knowing or realizing things about your own self may be what are keeping you from excelling at school, at your job, or even in your love life. When you stop knowing, you stop growing and whatever stops growing starts to die. Feed your mind all the knowledge you can, the mind is infinite, and so is knowledge, there is never enough.

Jewel 11: How to Avoid Being the Drop Out

This jewel may not apply to you depending on your age, but then again if you did drop out of school, it is never too late to go back to get your diploma. For the moment, I want to focus on the highschoolers.

High school can be an overwhelming experience. Instead of being a place to learn math and science, it can be a fashion show where everybody is focused on being the coolest and out swag the next person. Who is the toughest and most gangsta guy or girl in the building? The hallways become a runway for the models and turn into street corners for the blossoming thugs/thugettes. The teachers are relaxed and are not stressing the youngins to get to class, and if they do it is a lone teacher here and there. For the most part no one is going to stress you to be anywhere and you can get away with it.

Keep these next lines in mind if you are going into high school or any situation like that, don't forget what you are there for. You are there to learn from the teachers that went to not only high school, but college as well. Whether it is English, Math, Science, History, Foreign Language, or even Gym strive for excellence...how do you even fail gym??? Don't forget that you are there to earn a diploma, not be tougher or to intimidate your teacher or fellow classmates, or to be the know it all. Listen more and speak less; that is why we have two ears and one mouth.

I don't care if you have one pair of pants and one shirt, keep them clean and keep it moving to the next class. Never mind those who would laugh at your being poor. Just stick to your business of getting that diploma, then going on to college, or into another lucrative legal opportunity that may be available to you, such as the military, where you could receive free college education while also learning lifelong skills.

Knowledge is power and breeds success.

Never stop pushing to the limits of your abilities. Stick to the script and learn more so you can earn more. You will be able to look back on the haters, like how 50 Cent says in one of his songs "Damn Homie, in high school you was the man homie...what happened to you?" Chances are he or she got too focused on their own swag and forgot what they were in school for, and got turned out in the streets, street dreaming, chasing waterfalls. Don't let that happen to you, they have another building for gangstas to hang out in; its called prison if they are lucky.

Jewel 12: Pay Attention

This is very important; the person who pays attention is more than 99.9% likely, the person who gets paid. The person who gets paid, seizes prime opportunity first, and does not have to ask many questions. If you are paying attention, which means not just listening and seeing, but understand what you are listening to and are seeing, you will realize that people tell you what they want, need, like, and dislike one hundred times before they actually tell you blatantly what the problem is or isn't. Think about yourself for a minute, what are some of the ways you tell a person you are hungry, upset, or that you like them without actually telling them bluntly. You tell them through body language, eyes, actions, or indirect words. There's a 99% chance the other person does the same things you would do.

Get in tune with yourself, because to know

you is to know other people. We all have slight differences, but overall we are all the same. Pay Attention!!!

Jewel 13: Spot the Pattern

This also requires that you pay attention, because chances are if you are paying attention it is relatively easy to spot the pattern. One of the most obvious patterns that we all are use to is the pattern of seasons. Every 90 days a new season starts, 90 days for summer, 90 days for autumn, 90 days for winter, and 90 days for spring. There are 4 seasons times 3 months a piece is equal to 12 months, and that is equal to one year. That's a pattern, every 12 months a New Year starts, which is a consistent pattern.

Now if you are paying attention to the patterns of the seasons within the year, you will be able to know when it gets hot, cold, rains, snows, when the flowers grow, and when the leaves begin to fall off of the trees. If you are a man who lives with a woman you should be able to know the time of month your lady starts PMS, how your friend gets when he or she starts drinking beer or liquor, or the time schedules that the bus and trains are running or not.

If you're a guy and every time you come around all the girls start leaving, that is a pattern. You need not worry because the beauty of spotting a pattern especially with people or man made things like cars and houses, is that if they are broken, not working properly, or not what you like, you can fix them. You would just have to find out why the girls leave when you come around, including the one you really like, but first you have to pay attention and spot the pattern. Ask somebody why the girls do that, and then you can work on fixing the problem. It could be something as simple as changing your cologne, which all the girls think makes you smell like a skunk, but are too embarrassed to tell you. Next thing you know, after you change that cologne and washed the smell out of your clothes, they are inviting you out on dates. You could have spotted it sooner if you looked at the way their noses turned up when you showed up. It's the same look you give off every time your brother blows out a toxic fart. Pay attention, spot the patterns, and get to know yourself.

Jewel 14: Slippin'

You could be Mr. or Ms. Goodie Two Shoes, donate money to all the charities in the world, feed the homeless, care for the sick and elderly, even run an orphanage for abandoned children. If you get caught slippin' the whole world will turn against you in the blink of an eye. You could be the first one to work every day and make coffee for everyone, if somebody catches you with your hand in the cookie jar or thinks they see crumbs on your shirt, they will flip on you.

If you get caught cheating on your spouse, your relationship could come to an abrupt end. Doesn't matter how many I love you's have been shared, how many kids you have, or how many years you've been together. One false move and all you have worked for and gained could disappear just like that. I thought about this recently when I saw the Tiger Woods situation, he got caught cheating and not only lost his wife, but just about all of his sponsors as well, just like that. It didn't matter how much money he made them or how good he had been previously, in the blink of an eye all gone.

You could be the employee of the month for 100 months straight, get caught stealing and you are fired, maybe jailed. The point is that it can take seconds to destroy what sometimes takes years to build. A good name, trust, love, even life itself. It takes 21 years of living by the laws standard to be considered an adult...21 years. A drunk driver, slip and fall, stray bullet, to name a few could take that long journey away from you instantaneously. Even if you are the drunk driver or the trigger man, your life can be altered as well by being exiled to prison. It wouldn't matter if you were in school or peace corps, all the skills you have acquired that could help society would be rendered useless, because you got caught slippin'. So watch what you do and always think twice because you could be here today and gone tomorrow. You would become a statistic, who never reached their full potential.

Jewel 15: Do the Math

Black plus white equals grey; flour, eggs, milk, and yeast baked in the oven makes bread. Amor means love in Spanish, just about everything has a recipe or a simple this means that equation. You just have to figure out what they are, it goes like this: you eat junk food all day, sit on your butt all day, and never exercise; this equals you will be fat and out of shape. If a woman feels disrespected when someone calls her baby and you know this but still call her baby, she'll take it as you have no respect for her. Doing crime or being a gangsta equals death or prison, eventually. That's a recipe that many people have tried to change, but the results are always the same. Just like paying attention or spotting patterns, learn to do the math with people, places, and things; and you will be on your way to become a master of life.

Jewel 16: Overdoing It

Just like you can talk yourself into a good thing, you can talk yourself out of a good thing. Know when to call it a night, there is always another day. You would rather be 10% underworked, then to be 10% overworked.

Some people work out so hard that they over train, then pull or break something on their body. This then puts them out of commission until further notice, and then they can't get any work done. While the person who trains, but takes breaks and rest days, is still able to keep working. A man could be having an argument with his lady and could be overwhelmingly right with his accusations, and she may be ready to give in and apologize until the man may overdo it saying or calling her out of her name, this only leads to a new problem. So pace yourself or risk being burned out and rendered no use at all. Take it slow, take your time, don't be in a hurry, and don't OD. Remember everything in moderation.

Jewel 17: Belief's Cure and Belief's Kill

There's nothing like believing in you, having something, or someone to believe in. Such as religion or a parent, however you have to watch what you put your faith in. Belief is that strong! We are not talking about irrational beliefs such as, if you jump off a 40 story building without a parachute and believe hard enough you can turn into a bird and be able to fly away. No, it doesn't work that way, because you will be splattered all over the ground.

I'm talking about belief in the mental sense. Where what you want to believe in can be used to manipulate you and get you to do things you wouldn't ordinarily do. Love is something powerful to put your trust in, love of money, love of a significant other, an opportunity etc...Many people find themselves in tight spots on a daily basis because of what they believe in.

There's a person somewhere in the world right now willing to suicide bomb something because they believe their religious beliefs are the most exact and all those who would oppose them should die, especially in Holy War. It's no secret that I'm referring to Islam, only an example, right or wrong isn't want I am here to explore, only to point out the power of belief. I don't believe it is that serious, I believe a person should be able or has the right to do what they like in the pursuit of happiness, as long as they are not hurting themselves or anyone else.

I believe what you do to yourself is your business, to an extent. We have to be mindful of the effects that harming our own selves can bring especially if you have children, family, or even a pet that loves you. There are a whole lot of people who believed in Bernie Madoff, the Wall Street broker, before he made off with all their hard earned cash. Do your homework on whom and what you believe in. You wouldn't drive a car without a steering wheel, ride a bike without handle bars, or brakes; nor decide to swim across the Atlantic Ocean from North America to Africa nonstop without a backup plan. Mainly a boat and all sorts of other things that you realize you need about an hour or two into your swim.

People who believe that they can achieve great things usually do. The same with thinking healthy or sick, or the people who think like losers will lose. If it's all in the mind, get your mind right. Investigate what you put your all into, before you put your all into it. President Barack Obama believed he could win the presidential election and yes he did!

Jewel 18: Know What You Want

Remember in Jewel 2 when the example of wanting chicken but ordering a hamburger was used? Good, remember that scenario now as an example of going against what you want. This is the case with a great deal of people today; they want one thing but waste their time doing something else, opposite of what they really want.

Don't waste your time doing things that are counterproductive or contradictive to what it is that you really want or need to happen. If you wanted to sing you would not go to dancing school, you would take singing lessons. If you wanted to be a better lover to your significant other, you would enroll in some Kama Sutra classes and maybe even a poetry group. You would not go to the firing range to learn how to be a lover to your mate. That may teach you how to shoot a gun accurately in the event that you need to protect your mate, but won't make you sexually or intimately gratifying. Knowing how to shoot accurately would just make you a bodyguard, police officer, or security.

Know exactly what you want and go for it. If you want to be cool, be cool, don't be a clown. If you want to be smart, don't act stupid. If you want the sexy hot woman or the attractive sexy man, go for the person. Why limit yourself? This brings us to the next Jewel.

Jewel 19: Do it How You Do it

You can be short and fat, tall and skinny, big and tall, thin and short, have a lot of muscles, no muscles at all, you can be pale white, midnight black, high yellow, brown tones, olive complexion, red as an apple, or light skin. In addition to that, you can have curly jet black, brown, red, or blonde hair. It can be nappy and as kinky, thick, and wooly as Buffalo or Sheep hair, as straight and fine as silk, or have no hair at all. You can have all your teeth in your mouth; they can be pearly white or sunshine yellow. You could be driving a Bentley, riding the bus, pushing the hooptie, or riding a bike. You could live in a mansion or a rundown apartment. You could shop only on 5th Ave wearing designer garments made by top designers or shop at Wal-Mart and wear no name designers. You could be Harvard educated or hood educated, GED or high school diploma, or none of the above. The point is be YOU, I could be an alright you, but a great ME. Vice versa you would make an alright me, but a better YOU. Love yourself regardless of the circumstances.

Everybody in the world has a struggle that they are dealing with; everybody has to experience life in their own special way. Regardless of the age, color, location, or religion, everyone has their fair share of pain and suffering. Whether they show it or not, some go through physical hardships, while others struggle mentally and there are those that are going through it mentally and physically.

New born baby has to deal with the challenge of learning how to walk and talk among a million other things. While an older person may be fighting with the ability to continue walking, talking, and remembering in the midst of countless other obstacles as they get older. Treat people how you want to be treated. Respect your struggle and remember that pain and suffering define us. Do not waste time being jealous, envious, or hateful. Do what you do, play how you play. Learn the rules then play by them, and if they are not right and you can make them better, change them. Overall, be you because there is only one you and only one me.

Jewel 20: Don't Get Beside Yourself

I don't care if you have just made your first dollar or first million dollars, don't ever act like you are the first one to have made that money. Be thankful you got it, stay humble, and be mindful that it all can be removed from your possession in the blink of an eye. Staying low about your gains also keeps the haters at bay. I understand haters are necessary to a degree, to keep you on your toes. However, too much bragging, boasting, and gloating can be viewed as arrogance and being cocky. They will concentrate solely on destroying you. Always keep a quiet confidence that says, "I know I do what I do well, you know I do well, you are feeling the way I get busy, but we don't really have to talk about it, because this is just how I do things so it's nothing." Burn this norm into your mindset and you will go far in your business and personal relationships as well.

This is similar to slippin', constantly check yourself and remind yourself to stay low and focused on what is important to you. Keep setting goals to conquer so you don't get trapped in one victory, like an older person still stuck in the 80's or an old pimp still stuck in the 70's. This can be assumed as their "hay day," it was their hay day because they have not accomplished much since then. Never polarize yourself, keep upgrading yourself, and growing. Don't act like it is over, win, lose, or draw; it isn't over until you are dead. The game does not stop, you are part of life but life does not revolve around you or me. The sun doesn't have to tell you that it shines; it just does because that is what it does.

Jewel 21: It is What It is

A chicken can't roar like a lion, a fish can't bark like a dog, and don't ever expect to hear a rock fart then say excuse me, because it will never happen. Some things will never change ever, so if they can't change why worry about changing them? Let a tall person be tall and a short one be short. If you can't have something, why want it? If you absolutely can't have it, then don't want it. That acceptance will save you a ton of unnecessary heartache and stress. If you can't have him or her have a change of heart, let them go. You cannot make somebody love you or want you; you cannot make somebody want to do business with you if they don't like your proposal. You deal with every situation accordingly. People's minds and hearts can change over time, maybe in your favor or out of it, understand that. The winter does not decide not to come because you don't like the fact that it will be cold. Instead accept it for what it is and dress accordingly, or don't go out at all. If you can change a heart, mind, circumstance, provide food, clothing, shelter, or make someone happy, do it. If you can't then it is not for you to do or worry about.

Jewel 22: Think for Another or Others

Would you let a person who has had too many cups of Hennessy drive you anywhere? Would you let them drive anywhere if you could help it? People do the craziest things when no one is looking, when they think they can get away with it, or when no one says something about it. How about if you knew someone was building a nuclear bomb next door to you, would you speak up? Most people mean no harm or they can be extremely diabolical. They are just out to fulfill their own dreams just like the rest of us. However, keep this in mind; you have an unspoken obligation to keep an eye on those people, places, and things around you. In the case of the person building a nuclear bomb next door to you in a residential neighborhood or even in your apartment building, what if the bomb accidently detonates and kills everyone in a ten mile radius and you could have prevented it, how would you feel? What if you saw someone fiddling with the lock of the lion's cage while you were at the zoo? What if you saw someone trying to grab a poisonous rattle snake out of a snake pit that has no business doing that? What if a person was about to kill someone over something stupid like a can of soup, a male or female, or who was about to sexually abuse a child, what would you do?

There are countless other reasons to think for another or other people, young or old, because mental maturity does not have an age. Just because a person is 50 years old does not mean they are smarter than a twenty year old. Someone older might not be smarter than a fifth grader in some cases. A lot of people walk around with mental illnesses of all types on a daily basis who appear to be fully functioning, who in reality are not there at all. They could be literally out of their mind, high on prescription drugs with countless side effects sometimes worse than the prescription itself. Besides that with all the other drugs in play such as crack, heroin, ecstasy, cocaine, methamphetamine, angel dust, hash, mushrooms, acids, marijuana, even glue, and other substances. Let's not forget all the alcohol you can consume. To add to the list of mental blocks are love, financial, family, and personal problems, those could take a person far from where they need to be, could make a good person delusional.

There is no guarantee that a sober, intelligent person will make fire proof decisions any and every time they make a choice. Do you think a person who is drunk, high, or emotionally distraught would make sound choices? If you had a thriving business that was bringing in lots of cash would you let one of these types run the show? Unfortunately, some companies do have these types in charge. Even simple physical pains and sufferings can alter a person's mind state. A really strong toothache can cripple a person's capacity to do anything, let alone think straight. Disease comes in all forms and affects a person's rationality and patience. Then there is the real genius that would have you jump out of the airplane with no parachute, would use you like a pawn on their chess board. Expendable as if you were a piece of toilet paper they wipe themselves with and throw away. In some cases it is okay to be thought for; I would rather be a follower of the wise man than a leader of fools. Make sure that you are working with a clear state of mind with defined goals and objectives. If you are not thinking for yourself than someone else may be thinking for you. Instead of having your own blueprint you may be a part of someone else's, and their blueprint may not have your best interest or well being at heart. Good or bad, right or wrong, think or be thought for, or better yet surround yourself with people you can think with.

Jewel 23: Don't be a Racist

You don't judge a cow by its color, whether it's black and white, brown, or has spots, it doesn't matter. What does matter is the richness and quality of the milk that is produced. With people it's not the color of their skin you should be worried about, you should focus on a person's state of mind. Evil or good is not a complexion; it is a state of mind.

Terrorists have and will continue to come in all shades of the rainbow: Timothy McVeigh, DC Snipers- John Muhammad and Lee Malvo, Charles Manson, Osama Bin Laden, The Virginia Tech Shooter, The Columbine High Shooters, to name a few. They all represent different races and beliefs; however they all shared the same state of mind. Hate and destruction, regardless of their personal reasons for their attacks all have one; it was their state of mind that will forever link them together. Not their skin tones or religious preferences. We know good, loving humble people come out of every culture and walk of life. Whether it is rap or rock n roll, Christianity or Islam, Hollywood or the hood, the good, the bad, and the ugly are everywhere. Having blue eyes, brown eyes, green eyes, hazel eyes, red eyes, or black eyes will not determine which category you fall into or come out of.

Dr. Martin Luther King Jr., Mother Teresa, Gandhi, Jesus Christ represent different colors and genders but are the same in love that they gave to others. There are good parents and bad parents, responsible people and irresponsible people, some smart people and some are right out stupid. If you are going to be anti anything be anti idiot and anti bullshit.

Jewel 24: Don't be a Sexist

This one is especially for males but does not exclude females; however the main focus will be geared towards the fellas. I know the ladies are looking better than ever now, they are exuding sexuality, and have no problem expressing themselves through it or flaunting what they have. In some cases, even using it to get what they want. The Woman's Liberation Movement is real, not only do they want their civil rights; they also want those rights to be understood and respected. It doesn't matter if she walks around topless or completely naked, if she's an exotic dancer or the head of a Fortune 500 company she wants what any man wants, that is to be taken seriously. Having equal rights is mainly about respecting someone else's intelligence. This is not based on physical strength or how big you are, it is based on your intelligent comprehensive capacity to carry out a task.

Who is more mentally capable of completing a mission effectively, just because you are male does not mean that you are destined to be wiser than a female and vice versa. There are things that took place between males and females 20 or 30 years ago in the workplace that would have been accepted and overlooked. Flirting with a female, talking dirty to her in a sexual manner, or casual touches, however that was then this is now. Touch or say something to a lady in an inappropriate way and you could find yourself without a job and/or in jail. Some provocative words can get you a sexual harassment charge quick. Regardless of how she dresses or where she is at, you can still get a sexual harassment charge even at the strip club.

Women are demanding their respect. It is no wonder sexually oriented harassment, aggravated, and abuse charges are at an all time high. Some cases may not be that serious, but the ladies are making a statement. The point is to respect their space. Things will go a lot smoother for a man if he captures this point as soon as possible. Respect her rights and intelligence. If you really want to get with her, stimulate her mind. Where the mind goes the body follows, figure out what she likes. Most modern day women have no problem going after what they want including a man. Just because she may be gorgeous does not mean she is not on point. Don't let a woman's intelligence fool you into thinking she doesn't need or want a man. Treat a woman how you would want your mother, grandmother, sister, daughter, aunt, and niece treated regardless of how loose she can be. Males have a tendency to label a woman who has slept with different males a slut, skank, hooker, etc. However, a lot of males would still be virgins if they had to wait until they were married to have sex or make love. Most fellas are not trying to wait two weeks, let alone to get married. If you want a wholesome lady, get wholesome yourself. Stop throwing stones and labels around; remember water seeks its own level. Until then they are grinding just like you, so keep the head on your neck in control.

Jewel 25: Do Discriminate

It could save your life and I'm not talking about discrimination against weight, height, color, or religion, discriminate against certain mentalities. Evil is evil and good is good no matter what roof it is under.

If there was a group of people who only lived to get high, drunk, and break the laws, whereas on the other hand you are the type who does not get high drunk, and goes by the rules. Would it be in your best interest to hang out with that group? If someone wanted to commit robbery and that wasn't your thing or what you were really about, would you still go? Learn to discriminate against certain activities and mind sets, for doing so will surely preserve and keep your life safe.

Jewel 26: The Contradictions of Life

Just because the sun is shining bright out in the sky, does not necessarily mean it is hot outside. Just because it is a cloudy day does not mean it is cold outside. Just because someone loves you doesn't mean they will not hurt you. Just because someone doesn't like you doesn't mean they won't help you.

What is clear or white is not always clean or healthy, what is dark or black is not always dirty or sick. Just because a person has gone through school will not always mean that they are brilliant, and just because they don't have a formal education doesn't mean they are dumb. Just because a person is physically beautiful doesn't mean they are not dangerous or wicked, a tiger is beautiful but deadly.

If a person is physically unattractive, doesn't

mean they are bad or evil at heart. If a person is short doesn't mean they will be weak. If a person is tall doesn't mean they will be strong. If a man is fat doesn't mean they will be well endowed. If a man is thin doesn't mean they won't be well endowed, science have proven these facts. If two people are of the same complexion it does not mean they will have the same blood type. A black and white person can have the same blood type or any variation thereof. If a person is related to you by blood it does not mean you will be family to each other, and if a person is not related by blood doesn't mean they won't be family to you.

If a person quacks like a duck and walks like a duck, are they really a duck? If someone hears you, it does not mean they are listening to you, or even understand what you are saying. Learn the contradictions of life; everything is not always what it seems to be.

Jewel 27: Feel What Someone Else is Feeling

This jewel here requires a very open mind; you will mentally have to put yourself in someone else's position, predicament, or shoes. Imagine yourself in their shoes whether it be a man, woman, or child of any description, for instance- the devastating earthquake that shook Haiti and killed hundreds of thousands and injured millions. A person who wasn't there could easily say "better them than me," then keeps it moving about their daily business without a second thought. The person with the capacity to feel could easily think "what if I was in Haiti and my whole family just died, I've been injured in the destruction, I have no food, no water, nowhere to live, no clean clothes, and I am losing a lot of blood due to my injuries." Would I want someone to help me? Developing this ability not only allows you to feel someone else's pain, but also their joy. As well as what would help or hurt a person, at the root of things every person is just like you, and you like them. It is important to know how you feel, to know yourself is to know everyone else. Young or old of whatever gender, how would you feel if you were a 70 year old lady, with bad hips and knees who had to climb 10 flights of stairs to get to her apartment? Just think about how you would feel with bad knees, hips, back, etc…This is the road to feel what someone else is feeling, try it, and be flexible with your thought. You are tapping into the human spirit, a person can also identify with feelings or animals. Proceed with broad and deep conscious thoughts and feelings.

This exercise is not for the shallow or easily discouraged. This exercise can also help you learn and master a different language, and for grasping and understanding abstract and foreign ideas.

Jewel 28: Get to the Point-Be Blunt

With life being so short, be clear about what it is you want and need. Just like you don't want your time wasted, don't waste anybody else's time beating around the bush. If you had not eaten in 2 weeks because you were stranded somewhere, when you encountered your first person you wouldn't be talking about the weather or baseball, you would be talking about food and drink. If you went to the hospital with stomach pains, you would not start asking or talking about baking cookies. That would not help your real issue in the least. Not telling a person what you need, want, or showing them, could be the destruction of a life, love, and good relationship. Remember less is more and attention spans are short.

Especially in the business world where time is money, if you wish to play games, play sports, or get yourself a video game because there are many types available. In the real world people will respect you more and look forward to dealing with you on any and every level because they know you are straight up. Manipulation never lasts long and is as temporary as the tricks you apply to manipulate. Nobody likes to be controlled through shrewd and devious tactics, and once you are discovered you can bet your own skin that not only will you be despised but whatever trust there is or was between you will evaporate.

Don't get it twisted there are little games of give me this and I'll give you that, many play with their loved ones which may spice up their prospective relationships which at times can be unfair. However you decide to play it, make sure you keep it to someone who does it mutually and knowingly with you, other than that skip the idle chat.

Jewel 29: Be Nice and Show Some Love

Selfishness and hate will get you nowhere; forgive if you ever want to be forgiven. What goes around comes around, love, and forgiveness given, will be love and forgiveness received. If you don't show love, don't expect to see any in return.

There is an old story about a man who owed a king a great debt for using his land and was put in prison because he could not pay the debt. One day the king visited the prison and while doing so ran across the man who was put in prison for his debt to him. The man quickly explained his situation to the king who instantly understood the man's plight and just as soon wiped away the man's debt and ordered him released that instant. In addition to that, told the man he could live on the land free for six months. Needless to say the man was grateful. The king disguised himself as a bum, went out, and walked amongst his people, when he again came across the man who he had set free. This time he heard the man shouting and cursing at his neighbor over a five cent debt that his neighbor owed him, for which he borrowed to buy his wife medicine. Since the neighbor could not pay, he took the neighbor's only horse for payment. Seeing this the king ordered the man rearrested and reinstated his debt three times what it was. In addition, the man was sentenced to five years of hard labor. When the king again visited his prison and saw the man whom he had previously set free, the man asked the king why he had taken back his pardon and forgiveness. The king replied "why should I forgive you who cannot forgive." Karma is serious, what goes around will always eventually come around usually in three fold.

Jewel 30: Don't Stand in Your Own Way

The only person stopping you from moving forward in life or obtaining success is yourself, most of the time. Get out of your own way and head for the top. Do this by not being afraid of your own strengths or self. You are the help you need, help yourself so you can help others. You are your own strongest and most loyal ally, use yourself, and trust yourself. If you can't trust yourself, you won't be able to trust others, and they will not trust you.

There is always that person we all know who is always saying "I can't do this and I can't do that," even if we never speak it, I think we all get sick of that person and their inability or lack of desire to try. They seem defeated before they even start, if they are a part of your chain they are considered the "weak link" and a chain is only as strong as its weakest link. I don't think there is really an excuse for an able bodied person, not to be pushing the limits. Especially when we have amputees, paraplegics, and people who have other disabilities that are achieving on a daily basis, not just sitting on the sidelines feeling sorry for themselves, nor using their disabilities as permanent obstacles. An eagle can't be an eagle just sitting in the nest; it has to spread its wings and fly high because that is it's natural design and what it is made for. You were designed to fly high, but you can fly higher and farther than an eagle could ever imagine. Mankind has already flown into outer space and landed on the moon, we have gone deeper than some creatures of the sea could ever go. Run as far as you can even if it's only at a snail's pace, jump as high as you can even if you barely leave the ground.

Think as free and as far, wide, and creative as you can; it does not matter how deep you can go with your imagination as long as you go! Free yourself mentally and physically, you have the keys, you are the turn key, release yourself!!

Jewel 31: Have Something to Live For

If you don't have a reason to live, you won't. People find many different things that they claim to live for, their family, career, friends, etc...Ask yourself do you live for anything, is there one thing that you are passionate about, and have a deep commitment to? If not, then you need to reflect on things that have meant something to you in your life and build that bridge to reconnect. Live for yourself; take care of your body, mind, and soul. Start with that task first, live for yourself, take care of you, and then you will only benefit from then on. Once you have accomplished that task, then you will be able to connect or reconnect people, places, and things that mean something to you.

Jewel 32: Exceptions to the Math and Science of Things

No Matter how hard you try or how much you want or need something, at times things will not go in your favor. No matter how kind and nice you are, no matter how much love you show some people just won't like you. You can read all the books in the world; however some things you will have to actually experience for yourself, such as love, hate, triumph, failure, joy, and pain. Never be afraid to live, allow yourself to feel, learn from it, and how to deal with those feelings. One way to deal with your feelings and moods is to remember that, they are like the weather and always change.

Unlike the weather of our world, you are the master of your moods, and can always change them. If something is stressing you that you know is not worth the stress, simply choose not to stress. You have free will; mentally you can do anything, imagine the unimaginable, and unlock the power of your mind. Your mind has endless potential, think what you want, I mean literally. Don't be afraid to think the unthinkable, without rules or regulations. No matter how strange or out of reach it may seem, think the unthinkable. If seeing is believing, you must first see with your mind. That is where Dr. Martin Luther King Jr's dream began, in his mind.

THE ONLY THING YOU HAVE CONTROL OVER IS YOURSELF, SO APPLY THESE PRECIOUS JEWELS AND YOU WILL BE ABLE TO ACHIEVE EVERYTHING YOU'VE EVER WANTED!!

ABOUT THE AUTHOR

DeShawn Kenner was born in Mount Vernon, New York 1978. He was a hard headed youth who took to the streets. He made many mistakes along his life's journey and hindsight is always 20/20. He wrote this book to help others know how to avoid making mistakes by making better decisions; by sharing his understandings of where he could have done things differently.

PRAYERS FROM THE THRONE OF GOD

Prayers from the Throne of God

Garris Elkins

Prophetic Horizons
Jacksonville, OR
United States

Prayers from the Throne of God
© Garris Elkins

Prophetic Horizons
PO Box 509
Jacksonville, OR 97530 USA
prophetichorizons@gmail.com
ISBN-13: 978-0615455778

Cover design and image "High Places" by Anna Elkins

Printed in the United States of America

CONTENTS

I dedicate this book to Jan, Anna, and David:
my wife, daughter, and son whom I love so much.

FORWARD

The Holy Spirit is seeking to awaken the prayer mission of the Body of Christ: this book is a companion to the soundings of trumpets that are calling for you today.

The beauty of this clear-minded, spiritually pungent, biblical and practical guidebook in your hand is a tool, I believe, the Holy Spirit has fashioned through the experiences and wisdom of a pastor who has led a congregation for decades in diligent, harvest-begetting prayer.

I want to commend to you the faithful witness, work and shepherd-hearted character of Garris Elkins. He is a fellow servant I have known for years, and it is a heart-warming privilege to introduce him and this excellent work.

Never have I seen a more concise, yet complete, outline of dynamic keys to spiritually impacted prayer. The profundity of spiritual insight in

pivotal pages of God's revelation are presented here with simple clarity in ways that will enable practical application for leaders to read and God's people to incarnate these in their ways of thinking and praying.

Few books recently coming to publication have reached my hand that have seemed to me as timely and as truly igniting in their potential as this one. May the Holy Spirit use it to speak vitality and ignite joyful, impassioned and faith-filled prayer, intercession, praise and spiritual victory for multitudes.

Jack W. Hayford
Founding Pastor, The Church On The Way
President, The King's College & Seminary
Los Angeles, California

ACKNOWLEDGEMENTS

Books are possible because people beyond the author add to the process. I want to acknowledge some who have added to my process.

I thank my parents, Charlie and Lavert Elkins, who came from very humble beginnings. You showed me that God can take what the world considers "small" and make something out of it. Thank you, Dad, for telling me stories and helping me to see the power of a story well told.

I thank my pastor, Roy Hicks, Jr., for preaching the Kingdom of God and making me hungry for more.

I thank Jean Darnall who turned to me at a conference in Holland and said, "You will write for God." I did not know what that word meant at the time, but now I do. Thank you, Jean, for your obedience to the Lord's voice.

I thank Dr. Jack Hayford for modeling the life of

a credible and Spirit-led leader. Thank you for introducing many of us to the shout of grace.

I thank my daughter, Anna. You are a real editor and fine-tuner of text. Without your touch I am not sure this would have happened.

I want to express a deep awe, wonder and thankfulness to my wife, Jan. You see God in life. Thank you for opening my eyes to see as He sees. I don't know where I end and you begin anymore—we are truly one.

Jesus, I thank You most of all. You have loved me through it all. Thank You for helping me stay this course. I desire to end this life growing in intimacy with You and making the contribution into Your Kingdom that You created me to bring.

INTRODUCTION

There are many good books on the subject of prayer. I wrote this one partly to add to your existing understanding of prayer but mostly to increase your faith by helping you to gain a new perspective in prayer. My desire is for you to pray from a new freedom and boldness.

Gaining heaven's perspective in any area of our lives will change us. Without the perspective of heaven in our prayer life, we will struggle in prayer without a sense of victory.

God desires to add to our prayer life the power of declarations, decrees, and prophesy spoken from the throne of God over the issues of our lives and culture that have yet to come into line with heaven's intent. This kind of prayer does not supplant but rather supports the hard-fought petitions in prayer that some circumstances require.

As we unfold this perspective of prayer, allow

God to untie your concepts of prayer and raise you to a higher place—a place where you already live with Christ at the right hand of the Father from where you are able to shower prayers of victory down upon this life. This rain of prayer from the throne of God will release heaven's intent upon the earth and will soften its hardened ground in preparation for the new and extraordinary things God wants to do in our lifetime.

1

ESTABLISHING A HEAVENLY ALTAR OF PRAYER

Years ago, I was on a flight from Los Angeles to Seattle. We were flying thousands of feet up in the air over the beautiful Pacific Northwest. On this particular flight, I had a window seat and was able to view the passing countryside as it inched past my window. As we approached the Eugene-Springfield area of Oregon, a place we had called home for several years, I looked down and began to identify some familiar landmarks. The longer I looked, the more I could recognize streets, parks, and shopping malls. And there it was—our old neighborhood. I was fascinated that I could see it all from so high up.

There was the street where we had raised our kids, and there was the road I had taken to work

each day. I remembered our home hidden in the trees of the surrounding forest. From my high-flying perch, it all looked so different and small. My perspective had changed. My perspective changed because my altitude had changed. So it is with prayer. We only have a limited view when we pray from an earthbound perspective. Moving our prayer perspective to the view from heaven gives us the bigger picture that only this higher position can provide. We will see our lives differently from this higher place, and we will begin to pray differently.

We cannot always pray with confidence if we are only looking at what is taking place around us. What is taking place around us is not yet fully redeemed. Life on earth reflects a fallen world and speaks in an unredeemed language.

REPOSITIONING OUR PRAYER ALTARS

Our global civilization is in an epoch cycle of change. This cycle of change will test the things we know and believe. Human solutions will fail with ever increasing frequency because earthbound realties will not meet the needs of desperate people living in desperate times. People will turn to God for answers. This turning is what we have historically called "revival." In this turning, God

8

will ask His Church to respond to the world around us from the fresh revelations of His heart.

God is releasing a deepening hunger for prayer within His Church—a hunger for the language of heaven. God is preparing us to minister supernaturally in a world that is exhausted by dead religion.

A refreshing wind of God's presence is blowing across creation. This wind will clear our field of vision to see what God intends His Church to be.

One of the greatest, most culture-transforming powers available to the Church has always been prayer. Prayer moves heaven to bring its environment down upon the earth to transform the kingdoms of this world into the Kingdom of our Lord. Jesus Himself said that His house would be known as a house of prayer. The house of God is not a physical temple or a church facility. God's house of prayer is a presence-carrying people who are living and breathing temples of God. God dwells in this kind of house—in us—with power.

God is encouraging the Church to experience a shift in how and where we see ourselves in prayer. He is asking many of us to reposition our prayer altars from the place of our earthly struggle to the place of our heavenly victory. He is calling the Church to fully realize our position in Christ, not

only as a theological truth, but also as a positional truth and an experiential reality from which we can pray. We are being asked to add a prayer altar to our place in Christ at the right hand of God's throne and from there to pray the will of God down into our circumstances upon the earth.

Our concept of prayer is critical in creating an environment filled with hope and joy. We need to expand our perspective.

God has given us prayer to change this world through the transforming word of Christ. Your neighborhood and nation are waiting to be called "the New Earth." All of creation is in a perpetual groan waiting to experience once again the freedom it knew before sin entered the earth. Our prayers must also be created and released from the perspective of heaven, because this is where God is directing His Church in the supernatural process of the transformation of our world. God's perspective is our message to our world and our prayer for all of humanity. This kind of prayer draws from a preferred future that Jesus is waiting to usher into this world in partnership with His Church.

SEATED WITH CHRIST

The following story shows how this shifted

perspective works. A wonderful church faced a challenging experience. Their pastor had become emotionally involved with another woman, and he had stepped down from his role as the senior pastor. I was asked to come and speak in the church while they processed this painful situation.

As I spoke on that Sunday morning, I looked out over the hundreds of faces looking back at me, and I felt the pain and sorrow these people were experiencing. They did not understand this new reality that had just been dropped into their lives. They loved their leaders, including the one who had failed.

At the end of the service, I felt the Lord ask me to do something. One of the elders I had come to know was a fatherly presence of wisdom for the church. People looked to him for direction, and his words carried weight. I asked the ushers to bring the largest chair they had in the building—one of those upholstered, overstuffed chairs. I wanted something that would resemble a throne. The chair was placed right at the center of the platform in front of the podium. I then invited this elder up and asked him to have a seat. I told him that, as an elder of this church, he was seated with Christ at the right hand of the Father. I shared with him that none of the pain and sorrow had taken God by surprise.

God sees the beginning and the end of all things, including what this church was experiencing.

I then asked the elder to pray over the future of his church family from the perspective of heaven and the complete victory of Jesus Christ.

Something wonderful began to happen. At first the elder paused, not sure what to do. Then he started to pray, and with each word the intensity of his prayer gained momentum as he began to see this situation from heaven's perspective.

His tears of pain began turning into tears of joy. Hope began to fill the sanctuary. People began to speak up in agreement with his prayers.

God walked into the house that day and brought hope, because someone was declaring hope and prophesying a future greater than the painful shaking that was taking place in the community. Today, that church is thriving and living out the answers to that prayer from the throne of God, spoken by the elder. All of this was taking place as he and the church worked through the difficult process of restoration.

Revelation flows from the throne of God to the earth, not the other way around. Revelation does not come from brokenness; it flows from the fullness of Jesus Christ. The throne of God is planted firmly in timeless eternity, unaffected by

this life. This eternal perspective is a greater reality than the reality of this earthly realm. This earthly existence will always yield to the design and intent of God for a new heaven and a new earth.

God answers prayer from eternity into time. This invasion from heaven's perspective into our lives is where the supernatural events of God's Kingdom take place. It is a welcome invasion and one the Church partners with through prayer.

The Greeks have a word to describe this invasion of time and space by the revelation of God. The word is *kairos*. God's time—*kairos*—invades the developing line of chronological time. In these *kairos* moments, miracles take place because supernatural revelation has been released. Chronological time must yield to the invasion of heaven's will and perspective because a *kairos* moment comes from a greater reality than the one we are experiencing here on earth. Time will yield to eternity. Chronological time will always have to yield to a *kairos* work of God.

When we pray according to heaven's will and perspective, we begin walking in the intended authority Jesus had in mind when He told His disciples to wait in Jerusalem for a power that would fall from the realm of heaven onto the earth:

> But when the Holy Spirit has come upon you, you
> will receive power and will tell people about me
> everywhere—in Jerusalem, throughout Judea, in
> Samaria, and to the ends of the earth.
>
> —Acts 1:8

Chronological time is linked to the continuation of what is unredeemed unless it is interrupted by the redeeming purposes of God. The Day of Pentecost was an empowering of the Church, but it was also an interruption of time. When God breaks into our timeline and does the work of heaven, a *kairos* moment occurs. When this happens heaven's perspective invades earth's perspective and overwhelms the surrounding darkness. This is when revival breaks out and cultural transformation takes place.

In these moments, natural systems are interrupted, and supernatural systems of heaven are instituted; people are saved, the sick are healed, and spiritual frontiers are pushed back. Without this heavenly intervention, life would go on as normal. Frontiers of spiritual darkness are dismantled and pushed back by the revelation of God spoken through His Church. Our battle with darkness is about territory—the territory of individual lives and culture.

It is from our position in Christ, seated at the

right hand of God, that we gain a perspective of prayer that is infused with a boldness resulting from seeing this life from God's viewpoint. Jesus said that He only did what He saw the Father doing. The same applies to us. To pray the will of God means that I must first see His will and then proclaim it upon the earth. As Acts 1:8 instructs us, we are to tell people about Him (other versions translate this as bearing witness). Our boldness does not come from doing acts of obedience isolated from God. Our boldness flows because, like Jesus, we are seeing heaven at work. We step out in faith, and we speak what we see and hear.

In Colossians 3:1, Paul shared a similar reality with the church in Colossae, saying: "Since you have been raised to new life with Christ, set your sights on the realities of heaven."

SETTING OUR SIGHTS

What we set our sights on in prayer will direct the flow of our prayer. The reality of heaven, not the pain of our circumstance, is where we are to set our sights.

Hostage rescue teams train to rescue hostages and quell violent situations by developing tactics superior to those of the criminals. These highly

trained people practice with their weapons while hoping they will never have to use them. In their training, they constantly hear the words, "Focus on the front sight!"

Officers blur out the rear sight so that they can focus fully on the front sight and the target in front of them while still remaining tuned to their surroundings. Focusing on the front sight will direct the bullet to its intended target instead of an innocent victim.

We have been told to set our sights on the reality of heaven—the higher reality. When we see with heaven's sight, we are able to bring that reality to the untransformed parts of this life and demand them to yield to the will of God.

My wife, Jan, and I love our children. All through their lives, from birth to adulthood, we have prayed for them. Early on we knew the reality of heaven for each of their lives, and we prayed that reality every day. Our children would do foolish, childish things like all children do, but those foolish things were never their reality in our eyes.

God's word had defined who they were to become. We held on to the promises God had spoken to our hearts concerning our children. We have seen God's reality for them and have spoken that reality into their developing lives so that the

intent of God for them would become the driving force in their lives. We stayed focused on the realities of God's design and destiny for our children, and we see God at work in both of their lives. Maybe just as importantly, we have discovered God at work in transforming us as parents who need as much help as our children. One of our promises from the Lord is that He is turning the hearts of the fathers (and mothers) to the children, and the children to the fathers (and mothers).

The same principle of praying from God's reality applies to each person and circumstance with which we engage. God is asking the Church to see and then pray heaven's perspective into existence upon the earth. It is not that we are creating a new reality apart from God but rather that we are simply focusing on heaven's reality and not allowing anything less to gain our attention. Nothing is new or old in heaven. Heaven is eternal and timeless and so is the truth of God. Focusing on the unchangeable nature of heaven is a supernaturally calming experience because we no longer have to carry the weight of outcomes.

2

SEATED IN HEAVEN'S PERSPECTIVE

Places dedicated to prayer attract me. When I was a student at Multnomah University in Portland, Oregon, I enjoyed walking into the prayer chapel and sitting on the wooden pews. The chapel is as old as the campus. At one time someone proposed removing the chapel to make way for campus expansion, but the protest from past students stopped that plan in its tracks. Thousands of students have waited within those chapel walls to hear from God. It is a special place.

I can still recall the smell of that old wooden structure. I first visited it as a twenty-something college student trying to find my way in the calling God had placed upon my life. I spent many hours with God inside that chapel. Like me, hundreds of

students have sat in those pews, struggled with their calling, received life-changing direction, and answered the call of God to various ministries or mission fields. Others went on to make contributions into God's Kingdom through business, arts, and sciences.

To this day, every time I travel through Portland, I try to find time to slip into one of those chapel pews and talk to God. It is a timeless place.

Some of the heroes of faith we read about today started out in chapels and special places of prayer just like the chapel at Multnomah University. When we set aside a time and a place to be with Him, extraordinary things happen.

Recently, Jan and I traveled to Redding, California, to attend a conference at Bethel Church. During a break in the conference, we spent some time in the prayer chapel. The Bethel prayer chapel is not only appealing for its architecture but also for its expansive view of the surrounding mountains. On this particular evening, I chose to sit in a chair and look north. In fact I set my chair on the letter "N" that is embedded in the carpet as part of a compass that orients the chapel to the surrounding geography and beyond.

In my field of vision was Mount Shasta—all 14,179 feet of her majestic beauty. Mount Shasta is a

stratovolcano. A stratovolcano is a tall, conical-shaped mountain with many layers. These volcanoes are formed by repeated eruptions and coolings that give the volcano its steep slopes.

As I sat looking out toward Mount Shasta, the sun had already begun to set over the western horizon. The only piece of earth still illuminated was the summit of the mountain. The colors were striking. Shasta was reflecting the sun in a palette of salmon pink, orange, and white. The surrounding valley was already under the subdued and blurring blue light of evening. But Mount Shasta shone bright above this twilight in a proud display of glory. She was created for this moment.

Then the Lord spoke. He said, "Watch the high places." In the next few minutes, I would have one of those conversations with God in which He uses creation as part of His vocabulary. Our conversation was a combination of Spirit-led impressions and the visual display of what I was viewing from within the Bethel prayer chapel.

The color and light still struck Mount Shasta from the west. The east side of the mountain was similar to the colorless twilight of the surrounding valley below.

As the day continued to end, so did the light on the mountain. The shadow of evening twilight

began to crawl up the base of the mountain, encroaching upon the light display that had captured my attention in the first place. Inch by inch the twilight climbed up the slopes as the earth rotated and blocked each preceding angle of light. I continued to watch as the very tip of Mount Shasta hung onto the last of the sun's rays.

And then it was all gone. The show was over. It was like I had just watched a great movie and was left with only the film credits and the soundtrack music playing in the background. I was waiting for the "The End" to scroll up onto the screen and dismiss me from the theater. Twilight had erased the day, and now night was falling. The mountain began to dissolve into night as lights of human culture began to emerge through the darkness.

As I faced the darkness, the Lord let me know that if I would simply continue to look where the mountain used to be, the sun would rise again, and the mountain would display its glory once more in the morning. At that moment I knew what He meant when He said, "Watch the high places." When times are dark, it is best to keep looking at what God had revealed previously.

When we explore what it means to pray from the throne of God, we will realize that the high place, God's throne, is not affected by darkness or

the rotation of the earth. His throne remains above everything, above the highest mountains that we look at in awe. His throne is surrounded by the light of His presence.

When we understand that we live in a perpetual high place with God, we are taking a posture of hope and faith; we are believing that God is not Someone with a single cycle of promise, like a beautiful sunset affected by the rotation of the earth, but rather Someone whose promises originate in timeless eternity above the natural cycles of life.

OUR POSITION IN PRAYER

Comprehending the power of this kind of prayer starts with the understanding of our identity in Christ. Instead of always struggling upward in prayer from earth to heaven, we need to see ourselves positioned in heaven. It is from that place—being seated with Christ—where we begin to comprehend that our prayers can also fall down upon the life we now live on the earth. In other words, we pray from our reality in Christ.

In Philippians 3:20, Paul writes: "But we are citizens of heaven, where the Lord Jesus Christ lives."

We all carry a natural citizenship in our earthly

22

nations. When we become born again, we pick up a second citizenship in heaven with Christ. With that born-again experience, we receive the rights of citizenship in this heavenly Kingdom; we now possess a dual citizenship.

In my travels I have crossed the borders of many nations. My first passport had so many added pages that it became too thick to carry comfortably, and I had to order a new one. What I enjoyed the most about travel was returning home. Experiencing the uniqueness of a new culture was always something that added to my life, but home was truly where my heart lived. Because we are followers of Jesus Christ, God wants us to see that our real home, the place indicated on our spiritual passport, is where our hearts are most alive.

Jesus said that He was leaving this earth to go and prepare a place for us. That place, established in eternity, is our real home. We are sojourners living here, making Kingdom contributions on earth.

Paul gave profound words to the Church in Ephesus about our position in Christ:

> I pray that you will begin to understand the incredible greatness of his power for us who believe him. This is the same mighty power that raised Christ from the dead and seated him in the place of honor at God's right hand in the heavenly

realms. Now he is far above any ruler or authority or power or leader or anything else in this world or in the world to come. And God has put all things under the authority of Christ, and he gave him this authority for the benefit of the church. And the church is his body; it is filled by Christ, who fills everything everywhere with his presence.

—Ephesians 1:19-23

The resurrection power of God caused Jesus to be seated far above the turmoil and change that is taking place on the earth. He went there to rejoin the intimate fellowship He had with the Father and also to prepare our place in Him. When we gain this perspective, we will see into the invisible realm with the eyes of faith and then begin to pray heaven's reality into what seemed impossible to the natural mind. It is God's will that we be in His Son. When we pray the will of God from this heavenly position into the earth, we are not praying apart from God's will, but we are praying *as* God's will.

There will be a day when this old earth will become a new earth. Until that day a division still exists. Many of our prayers only reflect the earthbound half of our reality as children of God. God wants His people to rise in their confidence in prayer. This world cannot provide that confidence. That is why the writer of Hebrews says that our faith is anchored in eternity, not here. Our

24

confidence starts with the location of that anchor. The very need for an anchor indicates that the place of security is where the anchor has taken hold. In Ephesians 2:6 Paul reminds his readers: "For he raised us from the dead along with Christ, and we are seated with him in the heavenly realms—all because we are one with Christ Jesus."

Picture the image: God is seated on His throne, and at His right hand, Jesus is seated on His throne. The picture is one of complete unity and victory. Now, imagine that you are seated there with Christ. That's the starting point for your prayers.

Jesus emptied Himself of His divine privileges to come and live among us. Then, after His victory, he returned to heaven and left the incarnation in the hands of His Church. In one form or another, the Body of Jesus Christ has been on the earth continuously for the last 2,000 years. When Jesus ascended to heaven, He left us to be His Body upon the earth. The Church today incarnates the presence of Jesus. Wherever we walk we carry the risen Christ within us. The Church, living as the Body of Jesus Christ upon the earth, is God's model for how this is all supposed to work. This powerful, incarnated Body of Christ upon the earth is not the only place Christ resides. He is also seated at the right hand of the Father with His Church within

Him. On earth He lives in us, and in heaven we live in Him.

In God's mind it was not enough that we function as the Body of Christ solely with the limited representation that an earthly incarnation provides. The incarnated presence of Jesus upon the earth within His Church is an invasion of another and higher reality that we already live within—in heavenly places with Christ—a place where we now reside.

Heaven is always a greater reality than the reality of the earthly realm. When Jesus instructed His disciples to pray, He said, "On earth as it is in heaven." He did not say, "in heaven as it is on earth." The power of God connected the heavenly with the earthly. Jesus came and lived a real life in a real world. The incarnation of Jesus is the connecting point of heaven to earth and earth to heaven.

Many of us have limited our understanding of prayer to such a degree that we may be challenged by the idea of adding an altar of prayer in heaven to complement our earthly altar of prayer. Dual citizens who understand God's Word should not struggle with this. Our struggle is an indicator of our limited understanding of how Paul defined a believer as someone who lives in two realms.

3

THE WATCHMAN'S PRAYER

After spending time with God one morning, I turned on my computer. As I read the morning news, I noticed a live image of the White House in Washington, D.C. The image was a familiar one. Taken from an elevated position, the camera angle showed the flag waving and exposed part of the roof-line.

Most people would look at the roof of the White House and see it as just the roof of a government building. But I always look for the security personnel. And there they were: visible in the distant live shot, their dark uniforms in stark contrast to the white paint of the building. Unless you knew to look for the security personnel, you probably wouldn't notice them. These are the people assigned to keep watch. These are the people

assigned to look out for and protect against attack.

As a young man, I was a law enforcement officer. I was on one of the early SWAT teams (Special Weapons and Tactics) that were emerging in the law enforcement community across America in the 1970's. We trained with the FBI SWAT teams each month to learn their tactics. We trained within our own team to become a functional and cohesive unit. We trained on our own time to remain in top physical condition.

Watching the live video feed of the White House, I remembered working similar duty at Stanford University in Palo Alto, California. I had been assigned to outer-perimeter roof security for President Gerald Ford when he visited the university to speak. Roof duty is obscure and unnoticed to most people, yet it is vital to preserve life.

The watchman's prayer from the throne of God is comprised of a lot of "roof duty." You are on the "roof" of your family, your business, your city, and your ministry. You are scanning for threats that are only visible from the watchman's higher vantage point. Most people don't know you are there.

In the ministry of a watchman, you are not living in fear but rather in a state of prepared anticipation. This is duty you train for: sometimes

as a team, sometimes alone.

Parents do roof duty waiting up at night for a teenager to return home by curfew; they declare safety over a child's travel. A businesswoman works the roof when everyone else gets to go home at the end of the day; she prophesies turnaround and favor over her company. A servant-leader in the Church works the roof in prayer when no one else notices; his prayer covers others for breakthrough in the coming day.

Most of the people receiving these prayers will never realize they came from a watchman praying from the throne of God—the roof of heaven.

The majority of roof duty simply involves watching. In the Old Testament, the watchmen walked the wall of the cities, looking to see who was friend or foe. This is the essence of roof duty. It hasn't changed much today. The watchmen go unseen by those whose focus is only on what is taking place at ground level. To many, the throne of God is obscured by the troubles and pain of this visible, ground-level life. If our attention is trapped in our daily activities and duties, we won't be paying much attention to what may be approaching. If you have been assigned to spiritual roof duty, it will not be the job that gets noticed, but it will be the job that provides security for your

family, home, nation, and Church.

Whenever you find yourself alone on roof duty, remember that you aren't watching solo. God is up on the roof with you. God likes roof duty, and He loves to empower those on the roof with supernatural sight to see things from His eternal perspective and then to pray that eternal perspective back onto those living below.

4

OUR POSITION OF POWER

I pray that you will begin to understand the
incredible greatness of his power for us who
believe him.

—Ephesians 1:19a

The word "power" in Ephesians 1:19 refers to God's
power, specifically to the release of this power in
our thinking. This is called *dunamis* in the Greek
language, which is the root of our English word
"dynamite." Here it refers to the explosive power
exercised in the mind of a believer. The mind must
first experience the explosion of God's power before
that experience is translated into words that make
up our prayers. Paul used this same word when he
referred to the Holy Spirit:

And my message and my preaching were very plain. I did not use wise and persuasive speeches, but the Holy Spirit was powerful among you. I did this so that you might trust the power of God rather than human wisdom.

—I Corinthians 2:4-5

The ability of wisdom to transform human minds is found in the source of that power. Paul is linking the issue of trust to the release of power. What we rely on reveals where we have placed our trust. So then, what will we trust? Will we trust in the power of God that defies human wisdom and logic, or will we settle into a life of prayer that only reacts to what is happening around us? Reactive prayer is influenced by surroundings and emotions, but proactive prayers from the throne of God flow from an environment free of failing situations and human emotions.

Proactive prayers are influenced by God's throne and the environment of heaven. These prayers are crafted from the lexicon of heaven. If we are only trusting in what our minds can grasp, then we will only draw from the limited spectrum of human wisdom and power. The Church was never intended to live within a reactive mindset where darkness tries to set the agenda for our actions. God raised up the Church and seated us with Christ so

that we could function from the preferred reality of heaven. When we rely on the power and wisdom of God, supernatural things begin to take place.

A few years ago, I was asked to speak to a group of pastors in a nation that borders the Adriatic Sea in southern Europe. The area is beautiful and filled with the history of the Early Church.

As the evening meeting progressed, the leader of this national church movement asked if I would pray prophetically over the new church planters being sent out. As these leaders formed a line, I began to pray over each of them, sharing the words and images I felt the Holy Spirit was giving. I was working through an interpreter.

One young couple came up for prayer. As I prayed I began to see an image. In fact, the image was so real that it looked like words were being typed across the forehead of the woman in large print. I saw the word, "Occult." Not wanting to embarrass the woman, I leaned over and quietly whispered this word to the interpreter. He paused and then leaned over and spoke into the woman's ear.

As the woman heard the words she screamed and fell back into the arms of her husband and began to weep and shout out words in her native

language. I had no idea what she was saying, but I knew that God was up to something.

When the interpreter regained his composure, he began to question the woman. Several moments went by. When he got up from where the woman was now on the floor, he shared with me what she was crying about.

Apparently, this young woman was afraid of going out to pastor a church. The task of leadership was daunting. Her mother had been involved with mediums who predicted the future. So, at the invitation of her mother, she went to a medium to ask if their church plant would be successful. On this night God exposed her secret sin so she could confess it and be set free. With my feet firmly on the earth, I saw what heaven wanted to release this woman from, and her life was changed. Prayers that come from the throne of God will impact our lives in profound ways.

I have preached Acts 2 so many times that I thought I understood what took place in that upper room. The disciples came to the Day of Pentecost already indwelled by the Spirit because Jesus had breathed His Spirit into them in John 20. These same, water-baptized and indwelled-by-the-Spirit believers were told by Jesus not to leave Jerusalem and attempt ministry without the equipping of the

Spirit's power that was to come upon them—the power to become a supernatural witness.

When Jesus gave His disciples instructions in Acts 1 about the coming Day of Pentecost, He said that the Holy Spirit would be poured out upon them to empower them to become His witnesses, making them into a Spirit-empowered voice to the nations. Witnesses bring testimony. A witness gives evidence of something that has taken place. The witness of the Church for the last two thousand years has been linked to the initial outpouring of God's Spirit on the Day of Pentecost.

I began to ask myself, "What was the witness?" The witness was not only the experience of Pentecost itself but also the message the disciples were empowered to deliver. When we limit the Day of Pentecost to a set of experiences, we limit the full understanding of what I believe God intended that day to be for the Church throughout history. On the Day of Pentecost, we were empowered to speak the language of heaven upon the earth.

In Acts 2 the disciples were huddled together in fear behind closed doors when suddenly the wind of the Spirit began to blow. As this wind touched the disciples, the mockers in the crowd thought they were drunk. The noise and the manifestations were not the message. The noise only got the attention of

the surrounding community. The message of Pentecost was tucked away in verse 11: "And we all hear these people speaking in our own languages about the wonderful things God has done!"

The power of Pentecost was not only in the supernatural manifestations that took place that day; the power of Pentecost was the ability of the Church to supernaturally proclaim the wonderful things God had done in a language people could understand. This language is not always verbal. It can be delivered through art, music, preaching, writing, serving, and any area of life that is empowered by His Spirit. This empowered voice given on the Day of Pentecost also empowered our ability to pray with power and authority.

Let's return to a verse we looked at earlier, this time focusing on the word "power," the *dunamis* Jesus used when He said:

> But when the Holy Spirit has come upon you, you will receive power and will tell people about me everywhere—in Jerusalem, throughout Judea, in Samaria, and to the ends of the earth.
>
> —Acts 1:8

A key to understanding this verse, and maybe the entire event of Pentecost, is why the disciples were empowered in the first place. The disciples

were empowered with a new voice to witness. Jesus instructed them: "tell people about me everywhere."

As it is used here, *dunamis* is the explosive power of revelation that takes place when we speak in His name and in His power. This is not the delivery style or the presentation of a voice but the power that encases the words and delivers them for supernatural impact. When we are supernaturally empowered to speak for God, the hearers of our words will receive an explosive revelation of God's heart for them.

The purpose of the power at Pentecost was to empower the Church to share the wonder of God with supernaturally charged words that contained explosive power. This power would unlock human minds with the dynamite of heaven in an explosion of love.

In Luke 4, Jesus shared the reason He came to earth. His explanation directly echoed Isaiah 61:2: "He has sent me to tell those who mourn that the time of the Lord's favor has come."

Isaiah prophesied that Jesus was anointed by God to proclaim God's favor in the earth. The fulfillment of the ministry of favor upon Jesus Christ was transferred to us when Jesus was taken up into heaven to sit at the right hand of the Father.

Once He was enthroned, the Spirit was released into the Church. On the Day of Pentecost, the Early Church spoke in supernaturally empowered language, and when the people heard of God's favor, they called it *the wonderful things God has done.*

In Isaiah 61, a chapter describing the ministry of Jesus Christ and ultimately the ministry of His Church, words that describe God's impressive favor jump off the pages:

> Good News, comfort, released, freed, favor, beauty, blessing, praise, planted, glory, rebuild, repairing, revive, double portion, prosperity, everlasting joy, reward, covenant, honored, blessed

These are the kinds of words the people heard on the Day of Pentecost—words of favor and wonder from the God Who had once seemed distant. When spoken by the power of the Spirit, these words of favor would begin to transform the kingdoms of the earth into the Kingdom of our Lord. When we pray from the throne of God, we are speaking the words of Isaiah 61 into people and situations, and we are releasing this empowered voice to speak down upon the developing history that is playing out before our eyes.

God did not empower our voice to simply echo off the walls of a church building on Sunday

morning. Our empowered voice was given to us as a weapon of prayer capable of pulling down the strongholds of darkness that only look imposing when viewed from an earthly viewpoint instead of a heavenly one.

5

OUR POSITION OF AUTHORITY

There are social and political transitions taking place that will someday be traced back to prayers made from our position in Christ at the right hand of the Father. These prayers will not struggle up in human effort in some attempt to convince God to move, but rather they will flow down with anointing and set in motion supernatural change that reflects God's intended purpose for our world. Strongholds that many Christians have thought were too far gone for change will suddenly change. God is about to change what appears to be unchangeable, and this requires God's people exercising their authority in Him.

As a young pastor, I attended a meeting with a small group of leaders in the early 1980's in Billings, Montana. Jerry Cook was our speaker. He made a

comment that I will never forget: "Your authority will never be established until it is challenged."

Jerry was saying that we can claim to have authority, but its realization only comes through our response to the challenge of our authority. The challenge will reveal the condition of our hearts. We can become so consumed with defending our authority that we begin moving in a human authority that draws from a source apart from God. God wants our exercise of authority to depend on His life moving through us. A defensive life is a life that moves in limited wisdom and authority.

Jesus used the word "authority" when He spoke the Great Commission to His disciples:

> Jesus came and told his disciples, "I have been given complete authority in heaven and on earth. Therefore, go and make disciples of all the nations, baptizing them in the name of the Father and the Son and the Holy Spirit. Teach these new disciples to obey all the commands I have given you. And be sure of this: I am with you always, even to the end of the age."
>
> — Matthew 28:18-20

The significance of the words, "I have been given complete authority," is not just the process of making disciples but also the authority transferred from Jesus to His disciples. This word for authority

is constructed from two concepts. One is the origin or source of something as well the movement from that source to the recipient: from Jesus to the Church. The other part of this word expresses, "I am, I exist, I have been." In the context of this transferred authority, the word means the authority of the risen Lord resident in timeless eternity yet released and moving into time through the Church into the earth.

Jesus released this authority to His Church so that we could pray and minister in power. When we see death trying to raise its false authority over a situation or loved one, we are able to draw from the authority of Jesus Christ and speak life into dead situations. Such prayer is birthed, as Ephesians 1:21 tells us, "far above any ruler or authority or power or leader or anything else."

This prayer—effortless and throne-sourced—is not hindered by conditions here on earth. It is prayer that tears down strongholds that seemed immovable. Nothing is immovable to God. He can change what appears to be unchangeable.

6

Our Position of Intimacy

I have been married to my wife for several decades.
I cannot imagine Jan not being in my life. We are at
a place in our relationship where we honestly do
not know where one of us ends and the other
begins. This is oneness.

When we go to a mall to shop, Jan and I
sometimes separate to take care of different errands.
Even if I can't see Jan, I can sense her presence when
she is nearby. When I find her, it's uncanny. I once
found her in the middle of a flea market in Berlin,
Germany—a city of over four million people. I
hadn't even known she was going there; I had just
been out for a bicycle ride. She always smiles, "You
just know where I am." Intimacy and oneness are
powerful, unifying forces that overcome the
physical barriers of separation.

Prayer from the throne of God is an intimate act that senses the touch of the Father's hand because we are seated within Christ at the Father's right hand—within His reach, united with Him. Ephesians 2: 6 is not just a theological proximity; it is a real closeness and intimacy among the Father, Son, and Church.

I love the touch of my wife, Jan. When I feel stress, just one touch of her hand on my neck releases the stress. She says that touch is one of my love languages. I would agree.

Touch is also one of the love languages God uses to affirm His Church. Jesus is always within reach of the Father's touch. When God the Father touches His Son, He is touching the Church. Jesus said that He would never leave us or forsake us because intimacy with us is important to Him. Throughout Church history those who have been part of a great move of God have commonly said, "God touched us." Intimacy with God is a key part of the environment of revival.

Intimacy with God is a missing factor in the prayer lives of many within the Church. We make our prayer appeals to God Whom we perceive is somewhere else. For many of the same reasons that we fail to experience intimacy with people, we fail to experience it with God. We see our position as

not intimately united with Christ but only connected to Him through theology or liturgy.

Jesus changed how we are to relate to Him when He said that we are no longer considered His servants but His friends:

> "The greatest love is shown when people lay down their lives for their friends. You are my friends if you obey me. I no longer call you servants, because a master doesn't confide in his servants. Now you are my friends, since I have told you everything the Father told me."
>
> —John 15:13b-15

Many people still relate to God as if they are servants because they carry an Old Covenant understanding of God that was only a shadow of what was to come. In the Old Covenant, the Spirit came to people and then left. In the New Covenant, the Spirit takes up residency in a believer's life—and stays there. We are never without His Spirit.

The difference between being a servant of God and friend of God is a list. Servants work from a list of things to do, and when their list is done for the day they return to the servants' quarters. A friend has no list. A friend works from anticipation. Friends anticipate each other's needs. Friends understand one another because their relationship is

based on an intimacy that sees the heart. There are no separate quarters for friends. Friends are always there. Friends can walk into each other's lives at any time.

My father accepted Jesus as His Lord and Savior on his deathbed. My dad was a rough-and-tumble man with a soft heart. As a child growing up in the Great Depression, he had a completely different outlook on life than I had. I was provided for. Dad had to fight for everything he ever got. He was born in a sod house on the plains of Oklahoma in 1908 with a horse and buggy waiting outside in case the doctor was needed.

When he was as a young man, my father left home and rode the rails across America as a transient looking for work. He was a tough man forged in tough times.

I remember the morning the Lord woke me before dawn to go the hospital bed where my father lay dying. I went with the simple instruction from the Lord to read the 23rd Psalm to him. As I finished reading to my father, I felt the Holy Spirit prompt me to ask Dad what his relationship with God was like.

Then the Holy Spirit asked me to probe deeper, "Dad, have you ever accepted Jesus as your Lord and Savior?" The question was strange because I

know my father had sat through hundreds of altar calls in his lifetime. Most of our family thought my father knew the Lord.

He began to softly cry and said, "No."

"Dad, all these years sitting in church you never accepted Him—why?"

"I was afraid."

My father, the man I grew up knowing as afraid of no man, was afraid of coming to God.

Just before sunrise I had the honor of leading my earthly father in a prayer to come into a living relationship with his heavenly Father. What a privilege that was for me.

Because my father was dying, our conversation became very open and honest. I asked him what he wanted for his memorial service. He requested to have a soloist sing the song, "He touched me."

God touched my father. Touch is the condition of intimacy. God wants to touch us. Whenever He reaches over to touch His Son, Jesus Christ, He is touching those who are in Christ. We pray from a place of intimacy that releases prayers of faith.

7

PROPHESYING HOPE INTO LIFE'S MARGINS

Most of us have written something in the margin of a book or a Bible. As we read along, we jot down thoughts and observations in the margins of the text. There is actually a term for this: "marginalia."

Marginalia originally described the intentional designs in the margins of Medieval illuminated manuscripts. The margins of these manuscripts were filled with beautiful patterns and images in gold and silver that helped "illuminate" the text.

We all have a text that describes our lives. This life text narrates the successes and failures that visit each of us as we walk upon planet Earth. Along with a life text, we also have margins in the pages of our lives that have yet to be written upon. God has

words of hope and destiny that He places into those margins that illuminate His purpose for us beyond what the text of our life reveals. The Church has been called to prophesy God's heart into the margins of people's lives.

Paul described the purpose of prophecy:

"But everyone who prophesies speaks to men for their strengthening, encouragement and comfort."
—I Corinthians 14:3, NIV

The gift of prophecy was given to the Church to illuminate the life text of the people in our family, our workplace, and those living in the distant corners of this world.

Sometimes we don't understand the text of our lives. When a word of prophecy comes and fills in the margins, our life text is illuminated with things that bring us strength, courage, and comfort. Something wonderful and supernatural takes place when we know that God sees more for us than we can see for ourselves.

The stories of our lives on earth can be filled with turmoil. But we know that prayer from the throne originates far above that turmoil. As we saw in Ephesians 1:21, this elevated position is "far above any ruler or authority or power or leader or anything else." The social, political, and economic

strains taking place on the earth do not affect this kind of prayer.

Verse 22 continues: "And God has put all things under the authority of Christ, and he gave him this authority for the benefit of the church." Prayer from God's throne flows from the headship of Christ toward earth and will speak to areas in this world system functioning independently from God—areas without His headship. Headship brings order. Prayer from the throne of God will declare headship over the disorder and rebellion that is robbing the earth of God's joy. Prayer from this position of headship subdues rebellion, averts wars, and causes national leaders to yield to the word of the Lord.

As pastors, my wife and I adjusted our prayer life when we gained this perspective. We have the privilege of leading a wonderful church. We love the people, and they love us. When people walked in challenging seasons, it would have been so easy to give in to the fear a spiritual parent can experience. Instead, God asked us to pray His will over our spiritual children.

We began to declare the will of God over the text of their lives. We prophesied over their circumstances—all from the throne of God, above what was taking place in their lives. The timetable of change for each of our friends was unique to their

personalities and circumstances. What changed in our prayer life was how we saw the people God had entrusted to us. While we still knew that some were walking through personal challenges, our level of trust in God began to rise because the outcomes were not dependent upon what we saw taking place here on earth. What mattered most was our understanding of the heart of God for His people.

The nature of prayer from the throne of God is hope. And hope is sourced in eternity, not in time:

> We have this hope as an anchor for the soul, firm and secure. It enters the inner sanctuary behind the curtain, where Jesus, who went before us, has entered on our behalf.
> —Hebrews 6:19-20a, NIV

Whenever God has us speak a word of hope to another person, God uses our words as His pen to write His destiny into the margins of someone's life in a way that illuminates that life.

8

THE SOUND OF THIS PRAYER

When the children of Israel entered the Promised Land, ten cities stood as obstacles in their way. The first of these cities was Jericho.

In Joshua 6:2 God said, "'I have given you Jericho.'" Jericho was a promised victory. Israel was not yet a full-fledged army; it was simply a group of desert wanderers with a promise. Their physical resources were limited from years of wandering in the desert. Their only real weapon of warfare was their obedience to God.

The Church stands in a similar posture. We all face a Jericho that is standing in the way of what God has promised. World systems are unstable. Financial fear is trying to lure the people of God into its grip. But God is positioning His Church to bring down those walls just as He did in Jericho.

We all know the story of that walled city. There was no way in. God instructed Israel to march around the city once a day for six days. On the seventh day, they were to march around the city seven times, shout, and have the victory.

While I was a young pastor, Jack Hayford was one of the voices that forged my initial understanding of biblical leadership. Jack has always walked in that rare air of supernatural revelation that has earned him great respect. Jack once shared how he led his church in a shout of grace that changed the very atmosphere of his congregation. Grace is a powerful weapon. When the Church prays grace-filled prayers in the form of declarations, decrees, and prophesy, walls will come down.

The shout was the focal point in the story of Jericho. One-and-a-half million voices rose together. This was a shout of grace. A shout that said, "Our only way in is if God makes a way." This shout of grace was a desperate one; Israel had no access to Jericho unless God did for them what was impossible for them to do in their own strength. That is the nature of grace. Grace releases God's favor, and favor brings the victory. When we shout grace at our Jericho, God releases a supernatural favor that no wall of opposition can withstand.

What we miss in reading this story of Jericho is the size and dimension of what took place. The city of Jericho covered only six acres of ground. If you consider the outer fortifications, the size of the entire city was only nine acres in total.

At the time this event took place, the population of Israel was relative in size to the population of cities like Dallas, Philadelphia, Phoenix, or San Diego. Picture this: a city of nine acres surrounded by a circling mass of 1.5 million people.

The inner ring was comprised of the priests, the middle ring by the men of war, and the outer ring by the people of the nation of Israel. If you had stood on the walls of the city, you would not have seen a single-file line of people but rather a rotating mass of people reaching beyond the horizon.

For six days no one spoke a word. For six days Israel revolved around the city only once each day. On the seventh day, they marched around the city seven times. This was not a silent event. You don't move this many people quietly. The sound of 1.5 million people marching was powerful and loud. The earth shook. The dust cloud must have been thick.

On the seventh day, at the completion of seven circumnavigations of Jericho, 1.5 million voices raised and shouted at the walls of Jericho, and the

Word says the walls of the city fell straight down. This was no timid shout. This was an aggressive and prolonged shout as Israel closed ranks over nine acres of land.

Imagine 1.5 million people shouting and running forward, climbing over the rubble that once was the wall around Jericho. The former obstacle had vanished. This is what can happen when you pray from the place of victory enthroned with Christ against those things that will try to deny your way into your inheritance.

When we were young pastors, my wife and I pioneered our first church in a small town in the Rocky Mountains. Our young family of four had moved into a culture and climate that was foreign to us. We didn't know a single person. It turned out to be one of the hardest times and yet one of the best times on our journey in life. God was forming in us foundational truths for the years of ministry that lay ahead. Into this young, small fellowship arrived an older, more mature couple who were more gifted and more knowledgeable in the function of a local church than we were. They settled into a place of leadership. It did not take long for us to recognize that some things were not quite right, and we knew that we would have to address some personal issues in their lives that could eventually harm the church.

The husband's response was one of anger. In a private meeting, he told me what was wrong with me and the church. He then proceeded to curse the church and announced its demise. Outwardly, I responded as calmly and graciously as I could, but on the inside, I was in turmoil, shaken by the spiritual intensity of the moment. I actually got sick to my stomach as this man raged at me. I responded by saying, "We are sad that we have not been able to be of any help to you and your wife. It's important that you both be in a place where you can receive from the Lord. As you leave here and look to find that place of fellowship, we will be praying for you."

I went home and shared the whole episode with Jan. We could imagine the fallout that might occur in the church from this encounter. We felt the personal pain of that first shock and betrayal from a fellow brother and sister in the Lord. We felt inadequate and helpless to change the outcome for this couple and their influence on the rest of the church. We felt like we had failed. There was only one thing we could do. We got down on our knees and, with raised voices, we worshipped God. We declared His goodness, mercy, love, and forgiveness over the situation, over this couple's failure and ours, and over life itself. Our declaration and cry

was loud and sustained.

We learned some foundational things that evening about God's heart, about authority, and about warfare. Right after this confrontation, the church immediately moved forward in depth and character. A developing atmosphere of love and honor was felt. It was a turning point for all of us. Several years later this couple wrote me and asked for forgiveness. I responded with love and affirmation to their step of faith and was once again amazed at God's heart of love toward each of us when we are willing to respond in grace and mercy.

I learned something else from that situation. Our response is everything. Whether we are responding to someone who is angry with us or whether we are coming face to face with some immovable life obstacle, our response must be fueled by the grace of God or it will lack His power and authority.

The walls of our personal Jericho will not fall by human wisdom and reasoning. Another church program will not do it. Only the shout of grace in prayer will bring it down. The shout of grace in obedience to God was the weapon of supernatural warfare for Israel. When we shout grace-filled prayers, supernatural events transpire.

God is asking His people to position themselves

in unusual prophetic postures to pray prayers of authority in response to areas of life that appear to be completely closed and walled off. God is asking us to shout grace to the walls that stand in the way of His promise. This is not a timid prayer. It is loud and without apology. It comes after days of prolonged obedience in silence and marching in the dust.

Many individuals and ministries have been on a long dusty march, but now a plan for victory is before them. The plan for this season is the same plan for victory in all of recorded history of God's people: the battle plan is always a plan of grace. The cultures we live in are waiting to see God's miraculous provision demonstrated in His people. We are the ones who possess the shout of grace. The sound of grace is waiting to be heard in every city and in every nation upon the earth.

The prophet Zechariah spoke powerful words about shouting grace:

> "Nothing, not even a mighty mountain, will stand in Zerubbabel's way; it will flatten out before him! Then Zerubbabel will set the final stone of the Temple in place, and the people will shout: 'May God bless it! May God bless it!'"
>
> —Zechariah 4:7

Follow Zechariah's example and shout over the mountains in your life:

> ➤ Gather your mounting bills, and shout prayers of grace over them.

> ➤ Stand with your spouse, and shout prayers of grace into your future together.

> ➤ Shout prayers of grace over a wayward child.

> ➤ Assemble your ministry team, and shout prayers of grace into every obstacle that stands in the way of your vision and calling becoming a reality.

> ➤ Stand on the high places of your city, and shout prayers of grace over the broken and lost.

Once you shout the grace of God, walk straight ahead—right over the remains of fear and impossibility—and into your promise.

9

PRAYERS THAT DECLARE, DECREE, AND PROPHESY

Declarations, decrees, and prophesy are the vehicles that carry our prayers from the throne of God to people and circumstances where He wants to make Himself known.

What can we do when we have prayed through our prayer list and when we have called out to God? Is there something else we can do in prayer? We can begin to declare, decree, and prophesy God's heart from His throne into situations and relationships that appear immovable.

Before we look specifically at declarations, decrees, and prophesy, I'd like to comment generally on the power of the spoken word. We saw that 1.5 million voices brought down the walls of

Jericho, but even your voice alone has power.

God spoke and created the earth with His voice. We, His children, the Church, are made in His image and carry His creative voice. Our words can bring life or death.

When believers pray from the throne of God with the authority and power of Jesus Christ, our prayers can change the environment into which we are praying. Because we are God's children, we carry a creative familial voice that can replicate the sound of our Father's voice.

On the day of Creation, God spoke into the void. His voice was the assembly point for the elements to come and form the earth we walk upon. His word gathers and gives form to what was previously formless. For example, when we speak a prayer into the life of a child whose life is in disarray, our prayers provide an assembly point for God's truth to begin to work against unchallenged lies of hell. When parents intercede for their children, those prayers take up residence in that child, awaiting fulfillment.

Proverbs 18:21 (NIV) says, "The tongue has the power of life and death." What we say or pray will gather the elements of a life or situation around us for either life or death. There are huge consequences to our words and prayers.

I remember a season in my life when I was under tremendous pressure—the kind that comes just before supernatural breakthrough. I felt extremely fragmented. Into this fragmentation, God spoke truth to me that began to release the pressure.

In this particular time of testing, I had begun to speak words that contained no faith. I was speaking out of my pain and sorrow. I would have been embarrassed for anyone to hear what I was saying. I knew I needed to take a stand against the words that were coming out of my heart and finding life through my mouth. As I confessed my sin and my lack of faith, the Lord gave me a picture of what He was doing.

I saw an image of the Lord standing behind me. When I spoke those lifeless words, He swung a large shield around in front of me while He stood behind me. The shield was placed between my mouth and my circumstance. The words coming out of my mouth struck the back of the Lord's shield and could not go any farther.

Through an act of great mercy and grace, the Lord was shielding me from the words of death I had spoken. I learned that the shield of the Lord has two unique functions. One is to protect me until I realize what I am doing, and the other is to protect my future. I also understood that He would not do

this forever. He was giving me a chance to go to the root of my pain so that I could experience resolution and reconciliation. Through confession and repentance, I put to death my acts of rebellion and self-protection. I thanked Him for His patience with me and immediately began to filter my words to resemble God's heart, not my pain. My words had now become assembly points for the blessing of God instead of a self-created destiny of fear and death.

Keeping in mind the power of our words, let's look at declarations, decrees, and prophesies and what happens when they are prayed from God's throne into our world.

DECLARATIONS IN PRAYER

Declarations are like the trump card thrown down in a card game; they declare victory. When we declare in prayer, we are not declaring out of our imaginations, we are declaring the heart and truth of God. Declarations express the heart of God upon the earth.

When God created the earth, He said it was good. There is a goodness associated with what we speak because it expresses the goodness of God's heart and will. The nature of God is goodness.

When we realize this truth, it becomes "natural" for us to declare His goodness in prayer.

DECLARATIONS ANNOUNCE THE GLORY OF GOD

Sing to the LORD, all the earth;
Proclaim the good news of His salvation from day
to day.
Declare His glory among the nations,
His wonders among all peoples.
For the LORD is great and greatly to be praised;
He is also to be feared above all gods.
—1 Chronicles 16:23-25, NKJV

The word "glory" is defined as something with weight. God's glory, the essence of His presence, carries a greater substance than all the powers of the kingdom of darkness. When we declare the glory of God down upon someone who is living in rebellion, or upon a government system given over to corruption, our words will have a supernatural weight that will begin to crush darkness.

DECLARATIONS ANNOUNCE GENERATIONAL TESTIMONY

Great is the LORD, and greatly to be praised;
And His greatness is unsearchable.
One generation shall praise Your works to another,

And shall declare Your mighty acts.
I will meditate on the glorious splendor of Your
    majesty,
And on Your wondrous works.
                            —Psalm 145:3-5, NKJV

Revival in the Church is passed on when one generation announces the greatness of God to another generation. Many times we only see this as the older generation making an announcement to the younger generation.

We are in a time when the younger generations will be responsible for announcing to the older generations what God has done before. The fire in the bones of young men and women can ignite and remind an older generation who have sat back and given up on the promises of God.

Begin today to declare in prayer to all generations that Jesus is the same yesterday, today, and forever. He is unchanging, but His people must change from glory to glory. Declarations from the throne of God to the surrounding generations can become the revival catalyst for the next great move of God by simply making people aware of the mighty works of God in the past so that they begin to live in expectation of His coming in the future.

DECLARATIONS ARE THE PRAYERS OF A WATCHMEN

Prepare the table,
Set a watchman in the tower,
Eat and drink.
Arise, you princes,
Anoint the shield!
For thus has the Lord said to me:
"Go, set a watchman,
Let him declare what he sees."
And he saw a chariot with a pair of horsemen,
A chariot of donkeys, and a chariot of camels,
And he listened earnestly with great care.
—Isaiah 21:5-7, NKJV

Earlier we looked at the role of a watchman. What happens after a watchman sees the approaching chariots? He does more than just announce their arrival. Isaiah says:

O Jerusalem, I have posted watchmen on your walls; they will pray to the LORD day and night for the fulfillment of his promises. Take no rest, all you who pray.

—Isaiah 62:6

The great work of watchmen is not only the watching but also the praying about what they see. Watchmen announce the coming of an enemy, and when no enemy is in sight, the watchman prays. Without this balance of prayer, the ministry of a watchmen can warp into judgment and fear.

As watchmen on the wall, we are to pray and announce in earnest when we see the enemy approach. Isaiah 21:7 (NKJV) reveals this: "And he listened earnestly with great care." We shout and we announce and we pray.

DECLARATIONS ANNOUNCE NEW THINGS

> "I am the LORD, that is My name;
> And My glory I will not give to another,
> Nor My praise to carved images.
> Behold, the former things have come to pass,
> And new things I declare;
> Before they spring forth I tell you of them."
> Sing to the LORD a new song,
> And His praise from the ends of the earth.
> —Isaiah 42:8-10a, NKJV

The Church is the mouthpiece of God on earth. God announces His intent in this world through His Word and through the voice of His people as they are inspired by His Spirit. When God is about to do a new thing on the earth, He will announce it through those in His Church whose voice has been empowered with His message.

As we pray from the throne of God, we are announcing the new things God desires to bring forth things like healed marriages, prodigal children returning, finances made new, and churches

released into new seasons of destiny. When new things are spoken, hope begins to visit lives and cultures. Change is attracted to words of hope.

DECLARATIONS ANNOUNCE HIDDEN THINGS

> "Even from the beginning I have declared it to you;
> Before it came to pass I proclaimed it to you,
> Lest you should say,
> 'My idol has done them,
> And my carved image and my molded image
> Have commanded them.'
> You have heard;
> See all this.
> And will you not declare it?
> I have made you hear new things from this time,
> Even hidden things, and you did not know them."
> —Isaiah 48:5-6, NKJV

God reveals what is about to take place before events come into sight. The Church is equipped because God has revealed His will to us. He doesn't want us to be caught unaware, so He makes His intentions known beforehand.

Several years ago I was asked to speak at a conference in an Eastern European nation. This nation had been under the heavy hand of communism for years, and its courageous citizens had resisted with their own blood.

After one evening session, I was asked to pray and prophesy over people. This was a particularly long evening of prayer. About an hour into the prayer line, an older woman stepped forward. As I do each time I pray in this way, I waited for a word or image from the Lord.

A picture began to develop before my eyes. I saw one of those old-fashioned, hanging baby cradles suspended in air. Where there would normally be a rope at each end holding up the cradle, there was only a rope at one end. In the natural it would be impossible for the cradle to remain horizontal and hold the baby inside. With a rope at only one end, the cradle would fall down on one side and spill the baby to the ground, but somehow the baby was held securely in this image.

As I shared what I was seeing, the woman sucked in a huge breath and turned to the interpreter and began to cry. Smiles came across the faces of all who were near enough to hear what she was saying. This woman had shared nothing with me. I had never met her before.

Later, I was told that this woman was a grandmother. Her granddaughter was gravely ill and was left at home in a swinging cradle with the family so that this grandmother could come to the meetings. When she heard the words that were

spoken, she knew that her grandchild would be healed. God loves to reveal hidden things in times of revelatory prayer. That vision in prayer came from the very heart of God—from His throne.

When we live in intimacy with God, He will share things with us not grasped or known through the natural process of human intellect. In that moment of revelation, as we saw in verse 6, God is asking us, "'will you not declare it?'" Revelation is not just the truth revealed as a concept. The fullness of revealed truth occurs when what was hidden is now declared and when spoken truth becomes the landing zone where a miracle is destined to arrive.

DECLARATIONS CROSS INTERNATIONAL BOUNDARIES

"They shall come with weeping,
And with supplications I will lead them.
I will cause them to walk by the rivers of waters,
In a straight way in which they shall not stumble;
For I am a Father to Israel,
And Ephraim is My firstborn.
Hear the word of the LORD, O nations,
And declare it in the isles afar off, and say,
'He who scattered Israel will gather him,
And keep him as a shepherd does his flock.'
For the LORD has redeemed Jacob,
And ransomed him from the hand of one stronger than he."

—Jeremiah 31:9-11, NKJV

Once, when we were living in Europe, I sensed a need to pray for an older woman who lived thousands of miles away in the United States. The brother of this woman was well off financially. This woman was struggling month to month to make ends meet with only her Social Security check. I sensed something unrighteous was about to take place, and the Spirit of God rose up in me with an assignment to stop what was happening.

I began to declare that if this man were about to die that he would do nothing foolish with his resources that could dishonor his name or his sister's. I declared a stop to any ungodly decision that was underway.

Several months went by, and I received word from this woman that her brother had died. He was in his mid-80's when he passed away. In his loneliness he had become the victim of a woman who was setting him up to leave all his monies to her at the expense of his sister's future. I was told that within days of the man's death, his entire estate would have been given to this emotional predator. Instead, God stopped this ungodly transaction and left this vulnerable man's honor intact and his aging sister's financial future secure.

Declarations are not limited by time and space. When we declare God's heart and will from heaven,

evil plans are turned aside and honor prevails.

DECLARATIONS ANNOUNCE RESTORATION

> "As for you also,
> Because of the blood of your covenant,
> I will set your prisoners free from the waterless pit.
> Return to the stronghold,
> You prisoners of hope.
> Even today I declare
> That I will restore double to you."
> —Zechariah 9:11-12, NKJV

God loves to restore what is lost. When we declare in God's name the restoration of what has been lost, we set people free from pits of depression and fear and release them into the hope of restoration. The covenant of Christ's blood that covers His Church carries with it the restoration of all areas of our lives.

When God begins the work of restoration, He has in mind restoring us back to a fellowship with Him that existed before the Fall. We are not restored to the Law but to a place of grace. Restorative declarations send a message to situations of bondage that the shackles are about to be broken, and that what was lost will be restored with a double portion.

"Behold! My Servant whom I have chosen,
My Beloved in whom My soul is well pleased!
I will put My Spirit upon Him,
And He will declare justice to the Gentiles.
He will not quarrel nor cry out, nor will anyone
hear His voice in the streets."
—Matthew 12:18-19, NKJV

During the Los Angeles riots of 1993, my family and I were living near downtown where the riots were taking place. Several other L.A.-area pastors and I were asked to take part in a radio interview about what was happening. The riots went on for several days. The city was living in fear, and large portions of South Central L.A. were in flames. Through binoculars from our windows, we could see riots breaking out and looters stealing from businesses.

In the radio interview, one of the pastors, an African American, said, "When we seek justice that is not God's justice it is 'just us.'" I will never forget his play on words. Real justice must be crafted by God, not by human emotions or it is "just us." When we declare justice, we are not declaring our solution to injustice, we are declaring God's solution. God's solution for injustice involves

mercy, grace, and doing the right thing in a hard situation.

DECLARATIONS ANNOUNCE THE WHOLE COUNSEL OF GOD

> "Therefore I testify to you this day that I am innocent of the blood of all men. For I have not shunned to declare to you the whole counsel of God. Therefore take heed to yourselves and to all the flock, among which the Holy Spirit has made you overseers, to shepherd the church of God which He purchased with His own blood."
>
> —Acts 20:26-28, NKJV

In this poignant address, Paul is saying goodbye to the elders of the Ephesian church. This is one of the clearest pictures in all of Scripture of what a life well invested looks like. It was a sad day of departure because the Ephesian elders knew they would never see Paul again. Paul reminded them of their history together and said that he withheld nothing from them. He had delivered the full counsel of God.

Relationships and circumstances will arise in which someone is walking in only a partial revelation. The whole counsel of God may not be present. When we pray from the throne of God, we are announcing the fuller picture of God's heart and

intent for people. Paul did this in Ephesus, and we are called to do this in our lives and ministries.

DECREES IN PRAYER

Decrees are official orders that are transmitted by the representatives of a government. Those sent with a decree to proclaim will speak with the authority of the government that sent them. Decrees are backed by the power to carry out a governmental decision.

When sin held this world captive, Christ came and broke the power of sin by His death on the Cross and by His resurrection from the dead. A legal transaction occurred in the courts of heaven. When Jesus took possession of the keys of death and hell, He was acting from the legal rights He possessed through the victory He had gained.

When we decree in prayer, we are not bringing something up from our imagination. We are calling upon the legal rights of Jesus Christ that are now extended to His Church. We decree life because life was secured. We decree healing because by His stripes we were healed.

DECREES ILLUMINATE OUR WAY

"You will also decree a thing, and it will be established for you; and light will shine on your ways."

—Job 22:28, NASB

There are times when a current pathway has come to an end. We stand at the crossroads with no new road ahead. If we decree in prayer from the throne of God into these life intersections, God will light up the crossroads and reveal a new direction for us. He will make visible what was previously not visible. The decree will make a way.

When the Lord said that He was the "Alpha and Omega" He was saying that He is present in the beginning of all things and at the end of all things. He is light, and where He is allowed to shine, vision is granted.

DECREES RELEASE THE NATIONS AS OUR INHERITANCE

"Yet I have set My King on My holy hill of Zion.
I will declare the decree:
The LORD has said to Me,
'You are My Son, today I have begotten You.
Ask of Me, and I will give You the nations for Your inheritance,
And the ends of the earth for Your possession.'"

—Psalm 2:6-8, NKJV

For hundreds of years, this Psalm has been the prayer of many missionaries. When these saints prayed for a nation they were about to enter, they did so believing that God would give them entire people groups as their inheritance.

God has given the nations to the Church as part of our inheritance. When people come into relationship with God through Jesus Christ, this is the expression of our inheritance. The nations will be transformed and brought into the Body of Christ. We, as the Body of Christ, are expanded by each soul that comes into God's Kingdom.

We will literally possess the nations because they will become one with us through Christ, and we will become one with them.

DECREES SET BOUNDARIES

> "'Hear this now, O foolish people,
> Without understanding, Who have eyes and see not,
> And who have ears and hear not:
> Do you not fear Me?' says the LORD.
> 'Will you not tremble at My presence,
> Who have placed the sand as the bound of the sea,
> By a perpetual decree, that it cannot pass beyond it?
> And though its waves toss to and fro, yet they
> cannot prevail;
> Though they roar, yet they cannot pass over it.'"
> —Jeremiah 5:21-22, NKJV

The decree of God sets boundaries even in the created order. The decree of God set the boundaries of the ocean, and the ocean cannot cross the boundary of that decree. When the Church decrees the legal aspect of Christ's work on the Cross, hell cannot cross the boundary of that decree.

When we repeat His decrees, our words remind the created order of its submitted position to God and the people of God. Someday, when we enter eternity and see all things as they are, I believe we will hear of the decrees of the Church that literally changed the patterns of weather and the course of floods.

DECREES BRING ORDER

> Paul wanted him to join them on their journey. In deference to the Jews of the area, he arranged for Timothy to be circumcised before they left, for everyone knew that his father was a Greek. Then they went from town to town, explaining the decision regarding the commandments that were to be obeyed, as decided by the apostles and elders in Jerusalem. So the churches were strengthened in their faith and grew daily in numbers.
>
> —Acts 16:3-5

Paul prepared Timothy to minister to the Jews by circumcising him—a fully grown man! Then he

and Timothy carried special instructions to the Gentiles regarding worship. These instructions seem odd to us today, but in Paul's day these decrees set the Gentiles free to worship God and live in community with one another. The decree read:

> "You must abstain from eating food offered to idols, from consuming blood or the meat of strangled animals, and from sexual immorality. If you do this, you will do well. Farewell."
> —Acts 15:29

The Jewish believers in Jerusalem did not want to impose their understanding of faith upon the Gentile believers, so they sent this simple decree to them that applied to their specific situation. The order that was brought with this decree was not a legalistic decree but one that brought order by removing unnecessary religious weights from the backs of the Gentile believers.

When we decree something in prayer, we are releasing the order of God upon which all life depends, and what follows this kind of decree is freedom and life.

PROPHESYING IN PRAYER

When we prophesy over a life or situation, we are speaking out of current revelation that God is giving in a moment of time. These Spirit-birthed words have substance.

We saw Paul's definition of prophesy in I Corinthians; when we speak prophetically, we strengthen, encourage, and comfort others. As with the metaphor of the marginalia, we are to illuminate and edify people's life texts. Not only do the recipients of the word receive its intent, but the very environment into which the word is delivered is also changed. Prayers from the throne of God in the form of prophesy reveal the comforting heart of the Father.

A friend of mine in an Eastern European nation was a young church leader when communism ruled his nation. He had obstacles placed in front of him every time he tried to get permission from the city officials to do anything. The communist officials would speak harsh and angry words to my friend.

When these harsh words came, he would answer in the opposite spirit. If someone spoke hate, he would speak love. If someone was impatient, he was patient. If someone was not merciful, he would extend mercy. If someone was unkind, he would be kind. He responded in the opposite spirit.

Over time the resolve of the city officials melted

under the love of God that was exhibited by this young pastor. The city officials eventually granted my friend the access and permission he requested. Today, this pastor walks in God's favor throughout his nation because he spoke God's words. These words contained the encouragement and comfort of God's heart.

PROPHESYING WHOLENESS

Let's now look at the verses preceding Paul's definition of prophesy:

> Follow the way of love and eagerly desire spiritual gifts, especially the gift of prophecy. For anyone who speaks in a tongue does not speak to men but to God. Indeed, no one understands him; he utters mysteries with his spirit. But everyone who prophesies speaks to men for their strengthening, encouragement and comfort.
> —I Corinthians 14:1-3, NIV

The way of love that Paul asks us to follow brings people hope. Prophecy is one way that this hope is released. When we pray prophetic prayers, we call forth hope for ourselves and others. The gift of prophecy is not just for meetings in a church building. It is a gift that can and should be exercised in all areas of our lives, including prayer.

PROPHESYING LIFE TO SPIRITUALLY DEAD SITUATIONS

> Indeed, as I looked, the sinews and the flesh came upon them, and the skin covered them over; but there was no breath in them. Also He said to me, "Prophesy to the breath, prophesy, son of man, and say to the breath, 'Thus says the Lord GOD: "Come from the four winds, O breath, and breathe on these slain, that they may live."'" So I prophesied as He commanded me, and breath came into them, and they lived, and stood upon their feet, an exceedingly great army.
>
> —Ezekiel 37:8-10, NKJV

Prayer that comes from throne of God in the form of prophesy speaks to things that appear dead and commands them to live. When this empowered voice of prayer speaks, what is dead hears the command of life. Life has authority over death. Jesus rose from the dead because resurrection life is a greater power.

PROPHESYING HOPE TO THE SEED

> "Israel will remain a stump, like a tree that is cut down, but the stump will be a holy seed that will grow again."
>
> —Isaiah 6:13b

When I was a boy, I watched my father trim the mulberry trees that lined our driveway. When these trees were in full bloom, they provided a wonderful place of shade during the hot summer days. The first time my father trimmed these trees, I thought he had killed them. He literally cut them back to a stump and a few branches. But each year the trees grew back healthier and larger than before because within the DNA of the tree was a life and a structure that no amount of trimming could destroy. Life is like the mulberry trees of my youth; there are times when we get so trimmed we wonder if we will ever grow back, and then life happens again.

Once, when I read this verse from Isaiah 6, the words seemed to hang in the air. The Lord spoke to me, saying:

> I am raising up a host of prophets who will prophesy hope to the seed that remains in the stump. I never leave a stump without a seed. This seed contains the DNA of My life. It is activated and brought to life by hope. Raise your voice and speak hope to the seed that remains. The seed is waiting for the sound of hope. Do not focus on the stump. The stump only carries the seed. This present devastation is temporary. Words of hope are anchored in eternity. Rise up and stand before the stump just as My servant Noah did when I asked him to build the Ark. You will look foolish

to those who only see the stump, but I will grow the seed and the tree will stand again. Prophesy to My seed.

In my years of ministry, I have been able to travel to many nations. I have seen the Church worship in multi-million dollar facilities and in open-walled huts in the jungle.

In our Western cultures, we have discretionary time. This time is that extra part of our day that is not devoted to survival activities like getting water, finding food, and avoiding disease. In this extra space, we have the opportunity to read, play sports, watch TV, go on vacation, buy things, and develop the skills required for a hobby. Entire industries are supported by the existence of this spare time.

A consumer culture survives on the financial well-being of people who live and play within this discretionary time. When this time shrinks, the economy is affected. Talk to the car dealers today who used to bank on people buying new cars every few years, or the clothing manufacturer who hasn't seen the volume in sales he used to see, or the small-town business owner whose profit margin is gone along with the recreational shoppers who once made it possible.

Many people in developing countries posses one set of work clothes to wear in the fields during

the work week and one old suit or dress to wear to church on Sunday. For these people there is no discretionary middle in their wardrobe. Today, some of these people are not only found in third-world nations; they also live as the working poor in Western communities.

The cultural shift in which most of the Western world now finds itself is one of great opportunity for the Church. As the core of leisure time shrinks and the ability to fund that time also diminishes, many people will come face to face with a growing emptiness that can lead to fear and panic. Something must fill that void. This is the time for the Church to speak and pray into the emptiness and prophesy hope. People feel like trimmed mulberry trees.

Just as DNA remains in the stump of a felled tree, there remains a seed in each life felled by crisis. God is wanting to bring resurrection life to what appears to be dead.

As Isaiah was receiving his call as a prophet, the majority of the people in his world did not fully understand God, and they did not live for Him. That did not stop God. He was waiting to bring His love to His people if they would turn back to Him. It is the kindness of God that leads us to repentance. He always works with the willing remnant seed.

As you walk in your city today, God will bring you face to face with people whose lives resemble tree stumps. We live in a culture of fallen trees. God has sent His Church into the streets to prophesy hope to the seed that is housed in a decaying stump of human brokenness.

As the old tree stump rots away, a new season of growth will emerge because words of hope activated the seed within.

What does prayer from the throne of God look like and sound like in this context? It is made with the sound of resurrection authority because prayer from the throne of God comes from the other side of the completed victory of Jesus. It flows in opposition to the very things that stand in our way here on earth. When you see death trying to raise its false authority over your situation, run to your position in Christ in heaven and declare your victory in prayer from the throne of God. As that prayer is released, the kingdoms of earth will be shaken with resurrection power, and they will become the Kingdom of our Lord.

10

Praying out of Brokenness

Here's a story showing how all those declarations, decrees, and prophesies can come together in a single situation.

Early in our ministry, Jan and I experienced the deep pain of betrayal and sorrow. We were terribly wronged by the man who succeeded us as senior pastor of our church.

I remember the night we got the phone call telling us what this person was doing and saying about us publicly. There was no truth being spoken, only painful lies birthed out of his fear and insecurity. We were hundreds of miles away and felt helpless. We had entrusted this person with the lives of people we dearly loved. The words of betrayal wounded us deeply. I had never felt such a combination of fear and loss.

I hung up the phone that night, took Jan's hand, and said, "We need to pray." We got down on our knees and began to tell God all the pain we felt in that moment. It felt like our lives were caving in on us. It felt like someone had impaled us with a poisoned spear. Our guts ached. In one of those moments of supernatural impartation, God reminded us of the truth He had given us earlier in our ministry: worship in times of challenge. In that moment He released into us the gift of praise and blessing in the face of betrayal.

We declared that this was not God's plan. We decreed, based on the power of Christ's sacrifice, that this event would end up glorifying God. We prophesied in prayer over all parties involved using words of blessing and encouragement.

As we continued to pray, our prayers shifted into praise. We began to praise God for Who He was. We thanked Him for this deeper, ongoing training opportunity to trust Him in our helplessness. We thanked Jesus for this hurtful moment because it was taking us deeper into our dependence on Him. Then we began to bless our betrayer. Over the next few months more phone calls would come from confused saints about how this person continued to say horrible things about our lives and ministry. Every time we thought of

our betrayer, we made the choice to bless instead of curse. We declared a new outcome. We decreed from the court of heaven. We prophesied hope. This went on for eight years! Finally, it all came full circle.

One evening, we were invited over to the man's home for dinner. After all those years, he asked for our forgiveness. With great joy I was able to look him in the eye and tell him that we had forgiven him eight years before and had spent those intervening years blessing and praying for him. It was a joy to stand before him truly wanting the best for him.

The sorrows of life can wrap themselves around us to such a degree that, in order to survive, we must flee to our prayer altar in heaven and breathe in something new and fresh. With that inhale of heaven's breath, we are able to exhale prayers that will breathe life into situations that appear to be hopeless and impossible.

11

COMMANDING PRAYERS

For a year I literally lived in the Book of Acts. Acts was my year-long, daily assignment for study and meditation. Each day I studied the history and culture of that book. I soaked in its revelation and wisdom. Since Acts gives us the clearest picture of the Church at work in culture, I wanted to know what that kind of church looked like.

In that season of ministry, Jan and I were scheduled to fly to Athens, Greece to train a group of churches, and the Book of Acts was to be our text for those training sessions.

As I finalized my notes in preparation to speak, I noticed something. It seemed to jump out of the pages at me. How did I miss it in all of my previous study? In the Book of Acts, the Church *commanded* healing more than they prayed for it. This was a

stark revelation. I reread Acts with the commands of the Church in mind. I wanted to find the text filled with prayers for healing, but the pages of the text did not provide this kind of evidence. Instead of prayers for healing, I discovered that the disciples pronounced words of healing—they *commanded* wholeness.

When reading Acts 3 again, I noticed that no prayer was recorded when Peter and John encountered the lame man who was healed. What *is* recorded is Peter's command in verse 6: "I don't have any money for you. But I'll give you what I have. In the name of Jesus Christ of Nazareth, get up and walk!"

The disciples passed this man every day as they went to the Temple to worship, but on that particular day, the revelation of heaven came, they commanded that revelation into the lame man's life, and he was healed.

I noticed more commanding prayers:

> Acts 9:34: No prayer was offered for the healing of Aeneas. Peter just said, "Aeneas, Jesus Christ heals you! Get up and make your bed!" Instantly, the man was healed.

> Acts 9:40: Peter visited the dead woman,

Tabitha. He told everyone to leave the room, and then he got down on his knees to pray. He turned to her body and said, "'Get up, Tabitha.' And she opened her eyes! When she saw Peter, she sat up!"

➢ Acts 14:10: A crippled man in the town of Lystra was listening to Paul preach a sermon. When Paul realized the man had faith to be healed, Paul shouted to him, "Stand up!" The man then jumped to his feet and started to walk.

A strange excitement and anticipation began to fill my heart. God wanted me to realize something. The Church needs to rediscover the power of commanding prayer.

These observations about prayer in Acts are not meant to be some new formula for prayer. There really isn't anything new—just things that need to be rediscovered. What is evident in the lives of these early saints is that they ministered in the power of revelational knowledge. They were able to pronounce healing because they heard something spoken from God's heart: a discussion that took place around His throne. Something of heaven had invaded earth through the commands of the

Church.

As we learn to pray from the throne of God, we will need to cultivate our ability to hear the voice of God. Jesus Himself told His disciples that He did what He heard and saw the Father doing. Cultivating our ability to hear the declarations of heaven allows us to then declare the intent of heaven in prayer here on earth. God is asking us to pause to hear that specific word that will radically transform a broken life. From our position in Christ, at the right hand of God, we speak words that stop the work of hell. God wants us to hear that unique and specific word of healing He has for those hurting people in our lives and then to declare the release of God's healing presence just like Peter did that day on the way to the Temple.

The Book of Acts is the history of a Church that moved in the moment-by-moment revelation of God. The Early Church was taught this way because their model, Jesus Christ, prayed and ministered in this fashion. They ministered out of a revealed word from God, for a specific moment and circumstance, and wrote the history of the Early Church.

Some things began to emerge as I soaked in what I was discovering in Acts. These miracles happened in the daily routines of life. In Acts 3, Peter and John would have been going to the

Temple everyday at three o'clock in the afternoon. The lame man would have been there at the same time and place when Peter and John passed him by each day. What was different about this day is that God spoke a word to Peter about His miraculous intentions for the man's life. Once that word was spoken to the lame man, he was healed.

Peter and John could have checked the time of day and realized they would be late for the three o'clock Temple service if they stopped along the way. If they had yielded to the clock of culture instead of the clock of heaven, we would not be reading about this miracle in Acts.

As functioning dual citizens of heaven and earth, we need to shake off the "everydayness" of living this life and cultivate a sensitivity to God's voice.

12

THE POWER OF AGREEMENT IN PRAYER

I recently read the testimony of a group of young men and women who went to Disneyland for a day. After enjoying a few rides, they stopped at a food court and noticed a young man whose arm was in a sling. Someone in the group felt impressed to pray for the young man's healing and did so. When the prayer was over, the young man was completely healed and could freely move his arm. He started crying with joy because he was the star football player for his school, and his injured arm would have sidelined him for the upcoming season.

For the next four hours, over one hundred people lined up in this food court at Disneyland and got healed through the prayers of a group of young

men and women who stepped out in faith. An equal number of people gave their hearts to Jesus because they saw the power of God. It all started because someone followed the nudge of God's Spirit to pray. The "Happiest Place on Earth" became its namesake when God showed up in power.

The release of God's presence and power through prayer takes place when we come into agreement with the will of God. When we pray in agreement with God's will, His supernatural power is released into areas not accessible by human logic and reasoning. The continual and persistent prayers of the Church are the battering rams of heaven.

In the Azusa Street Revival of the early twentieth century, a small group of believers gathered for months to seek the face of God in prayer. They had a passion to pursue God, and that passion worked its way out into fervent prayer that called down the power of God into a building once used as a livery stable.

Frank Bartleman, one of the leaders at Azusa Street, wrote to Evan Roberts during the Welsh Revival to get instructions on how to experience an outpouring of God in Los Angeles. Roberts advised gathering those willing to surrender, praying together daily, and believing God's blessings. Bartleman followed this advice, and history proves

what happens when people gather to pray for God to make Himself known.

Jesus taught His disciples about the power of agreement in prayer:

> Then, teaching them more about prayer, he used this illustration: "Suppose you went to a friend's house at midnight, wanting to borrow three loaves of bread. You would say to him, 'A friend of mine has just arrived for a visit, and I have nothing for him to eat.' He would call out from his bedroom, 'Don't bother me. The door is locked for the night, and we are all in bed. I can't help you this time.' But I tell you this—though he won't do it as a friend, if you keep knocking long enough, he will get up and give you what you want so his reputation won't be damaged. And so I tell you, keep on asking, and you will be given what you ask for. Keep on looking, and you will find. Keep on knocking, and the door will be opened. For everyone who asks, receives. Everyone who seeks, finds. And the door is opened to everyone who knocks."
>
> —Luke 11:5-10

It is easy to study the mechanics of prayer and create a methodology for it. When we do this, we can forget what actually motivates people to pray— the need for results. To pray without the hope of God showing up and actually doing something will

soon shift our praying into a labor-intensive effort where the answers fall back onto us for fulfillment. At this point we burn out, and the joy of prayer lifts.

CLOSED DOORS WILL OPEN WHEN WE PRAY

Jesus' teaching in Luke 11:8 gives us insight into what happens when we pray: "if you keep knocking long enough, he will get up and give you what you want." When we seek God and knock, closed doors will open.

The illustration Jesus uses here needs to be seen in the context of the culture at the time He spoke. The image is of a home all closed up for the night. In the Middle East during that period, people left their doors open all day long, but at night the family and livestock would bed down in their one-room home. At night this single living space was crowded and easily disturbed. Any knock at the door would wake up everyone and everything in the house. When the door closed at night, it was only opened for emergencies.

When God answers persistent prayer, doors will open that may even violate cultural norms. This kind of prayer greases the hinges of obstacles and swings them open to access the realm of heaven.

When heaven is manifested upon the earth, supernatural things begin to take place, like star athletes getting healed at Disneyland or someone being healed in the check-out line at your local supermarket.

In the Azusa Street Revival, those who chronicled the miracles said that when the church would begin to sing in the Spirit, the manifestation of miracles, signs, and wonders would increase. These prayers, when sung in the language of heaven, opened up access into the heavenlies, and what was hovering above the prayers fell into the midst of those gathered. Sometimes we don't know how to pray, but the Holy Spirit does. We simply partner with Him in agreement.

SUPERNATURAL PROVISION WILL COME WHEN WE PRAY

Jesus said, "For everyone who asks, receives. Everyone who seeks, finds. And to everyone who knocks, the door will be opened." Notice the repetition of "everyone."

Jesus used the persistent prayer of the friend to release the bread of heaven. Like the manna, the bread came because God was the only One who could provide it. The bread of answered prayer

exists behind doors only opened in agreement with God's will.

So much of what is missed in understanding prayer has to do with our perception of God. Jesus ended his illustration of continual knocking by saying:

> "You fathers—if your children ask for a fish, do you give them a snake instead? Or if they ask for an egg, do you give them a scorpion? Of course not! If you sinful people know how to give good gifts to your children, how much more will your heavenly Father give the Holy Spirit to those who ask him."
>
> —Luke 11:11-13

The word "confession" means "agreement." When we confess our sins, we are agreeing with God that something is sin. The ability to see is the first step toward wholeness. The act of agreement applies to all areas of life, not just sin. Once our understanding about anything comes into agreement with what God is seeing, whether it is confession of sin or asking and knocking in prayer, real change is then possible. This is why so much of prayer is about seeing what God sees.

The act of confessing truth in prayer even effects how we see God Himself. In this process of revelation, we will begin to see the Father

differently. We will see Him as Someone who wants to bring His goodness into our lives. As we confess His goodness in prayer, our spiritual eyes are opened to see His heart and purposes more clearly.

We need to avoid reducing God to someone who only gives to us based on how good we think we are. If we make that deduction, we are saying that our actions change His character. God's character is intact and unchangeable. He is good and will remain good throughout all eternity. He is good, not because we fully understand prayer; He is good because He can be nothing else but good. God loves to open doors for us if we will come into agreement with Him.

13

LIVING IN THE "GREEN LIGHT" OF GOD

Several years ago, Jan and I had the privilege of having lunch with David and Deborah Crone who pastor The Mission, a church in Vacaville, California. When I get together with leaders like the Crones, I often ask what guides them in their ministry. When I asked David this question, without hesitation he said, "We live in the green light of God."

David's words deeply impacted my spirit. An adjustment of my life paradigm occurred as David's words hung over the lunch table. Deborah added to David's comment by saying that God is faithful to give us the red lights when we need to stop if we will simply live in His green light. As Jan and I

drove home after lunch, David's words began to rearrange certain areas of my life and ministry. I knew I had received an impartation of truth.

Some of our prayer lives resemble beautiful and powerful automobiles that are running at idle while waiting at an intersection, even though the light is green. It has been "green and go" since the Day of Pentecost, yet some of us still wait, continuing to idle and going nowhere. I sense that God is asking His Church, "What are you waiting for?" The reality is that the heavens are open, and the Spirit has been given to us. We are seated in heaven at the right hand of the Father on purpose. The green light of God is present in His people. It is time to invite the Holy Spirit to reveal why some of us are stopped instead of moving forward. It is also time to renew our minds and begin to live as people positioned by God to do more than just wait at intersections and idle our engines of faith.

Many of us have forgotten that we really are children of the Most High God. We have allowed lies to remain embedded and unchallenged in our lives. We have created a performance-based relationship with the Grace-Giver. We live in fear of failure, and so we avoid stepping out in faith, thinking that failure means rejection. Some of us are afraid to move forward in boldness because we still

believe that God can only love us if our performance is without fault. This fear has immobilized the prayer of faith in some; it blinds us to the green light and keeps us from pressing down on the accelerator pedal and moving forward. We displace this lie by remembering that we are loved not as the result of our performance but out of the very nature of God. He can only love. He is love. He is unchangeable in His love.

Fear of failure and rejection can redirect the focus of our prayer back onto self, and when this happens we become the ones responsible for the results of what we have prayed. We take on the burden of outcomes. "What if I pray and the person is not healed?" "What if I turn to the table behind me, say the word You asked me to give, and they reject it?" If we feel that we are responsible for the results of our faith, we will inevitably live in the prison of performance because the perceived power source is with us and not with God. This prison holds our life and faith captive to personal doubt instead of the open road of freedom that comes from living in the green light of God.

In John 15 Jesus said that He would no longer relate to His disciples as servants. He would now relate to them as friends. The shift here was not simply about using a new word to describe their

relationship but rather how being a friend would radically change the way the disciples would relate to Jesus in the future.

Remember: servants live with a list of things to do. Servants execute lists of performance, and when they are done performing, they go back to the servants' quarters. A friend is different. A friend lives in anticipation of what their friend desires. They have a relationship that is powered by intimacy and union. They see an open road and the green light of relationship and freedom.

ALL THE PROMISES ARE "YES"

> As surely as God is true, I am not that sort of person. My yes means yes because Jesus Christ, the Son of God, never wavers between yes and no. He is the one whom Timothy, Silas, and I preached to you, and he is the divine Yes—God's affirmation. For all of God's promises have been fulfilled in him. That is why we say "Amen" when we give glory to God through Christ.
> —II Corinthians 1:18-20

This kind of friendship with God that Paul described, and its resulting prayer, looks reckless to people who have yet to realize His friendship. Friendship with God looks reckless because you

end up blasting past people who are still parked at the intersection with their foot on the brakes. Friends of God travel right through intersections because they are fulfilling the anticipated desires of the Master: living in the green light of God.

In the area of Oregon where I live, the police and fire vehicles are equipped with transmitting units that send signals ahead of them to change traffic lights from red to green so that the responding public safety personnel can reach the emergency site unimpeded. The vehicles carry with them the ability to change the function of the traffic light. You and I carry the presence of Jesus Christ. That presence changes everything.

Followers of Jesus Christ live in the green light of God's promises. All of God's promises are "yes." "Promise" is a word that can be translated "to announce upon." Jesus told the disciples in Luke 24: 49, "And now I will send the Holy Spirit, just as my Father promised. But stay here in the city until the Holy Spirit comes and fills you with power from heaven." When Jesus said these words, He was assuring His disciples that in the near future God would "announce upon them" the Spirit.

The prophet Joel announced the promise of the future outpouring of the Spirit in the latter days. On the Day of Pentecost, timeless eternity announced

the reality of Joel's prophecy down upon earth.

Right now, God is announcing His promises upon the earth through His Church. This really is a new day. The fires of revival are sparking and igniting upon the earth on every continent. The promise of God has been announced to us, His friends, and we are the chosen voices of heaven to speak truth into our world by believing that all the promises are "yes" in Christ and by speaking that "yes" into a fearful and hesitant world.

14

A MATTER OF TIMING

The other day, I watched a television program about modern technology. The narrator described a new breed of missiles that have the ability to loiter; they can be flown to a distant location and then circle around until it is time to strike their intended target. Up to that point I had always thought "loitering" was a form of prohibited hanging out. In the small town where I grew up, the local policeman would walk up to groups of kids standing beneath the "No Loitering Allowed" signs and tell them, "move along."

Modern missiles loiter. They can now be launched from hundreds of miles away and sent into a targeted region before an attack begins. Computer-savvy warriors fly these missiles in a way similar to someone using a joystick to play a

video game. Once the missiles arrive in the targeted region, they simply fly around in circles, loitering behind a nearby mountain just out of range of the enemy radar. When the time is right and the target is acquired, a new command is sent to the on-board computer, and the "smart" missiles fly over the mountain and into the adjacent valley, destroying the target. Depending on the fuel economy mode, some of these missiles can do this for hours—even days—if needed.

When I heard of this futuristic weaponry, I thought of prayer. Many of us pray for the immediate needs of our families and ministries: the things we see and feel. But have you considered that God has us pray for future battles? In future battles, places where our lives have yet to arrive on a distant battlefield, our current prayers are being sent up into eternity to loiter until the time when the Commander of our faith releases them into a future target. As the Spirit prompts us to pray, our prayers are gathered. Then, in God's perfect battle plan, they are delivered back into time in a massive onslaught against the encampments of hell. Our prayers wait for the voice of the Lord to deliver their payload of victory.

Revelation describes an end-time scenario that speaks of stored prayers released at a later date:

And as he took the scroll, the four living beings and the twenty-four elders fell down before the Lamb. Each one had a harp, and they held gold bowls filled with incense—the prayers of God's people!

—Revelation 5:8

Some of the prayers that will be released in Revelation 5 will be thousands of years old. You and I are praying some of those prayers right now from both earth and the throne of God. In these golden bowls are the prayers of the Apostle Paul and other believers from the Early Church. In these golden bowls are the prayers of the persecuted Church of today coming from a distant village deep inside China. The bowls in heaven contain prayers that span thousands of years of Kingdom history.

In the Book of Joshua, the great warrior himself is about to die. He is reviewing Israel's history and future with God and how their battles will be fought. Speaking for the Lord, Joshua said:

And I sent hornets ahead of you to drive out the two kings of the Amorites. It was not your swords or bows that brought you victory. I gave you land you had not worked for, and I gave you cities you did not build—the cities in which you are now living. I gave you vineyards and olive groves for food, though you did not plant them.

—Joshua 24:12-13

Maybe this is what Paul was talking about when he told us to put on our spiritual battle garb and simply stand. You and I may show up on a battlefield dressed for war with a sword and a shield, but the battle always belongs to the Lord.

Throughout history, the Church has walked among the ruins of hell's encampment knowing that God had already gone before them and destroyed the enemy. We will also walk into these similar places of victory. We will realize that the prayers of our ancestors have been poured out upon our impossible situations. We will be humbled and amazed at what we see around us.

Can you imagine what it will be like to know that many of us are about to walk onto battlefields where we will see the enemy already devastated? Many will walk into the shattered encampments of hell and know that something supernatural has visited the battlefield prior to their arrival. The prayers sent into a future battle had loitered until the timing of God was complete, and then a victory came.

When God makes a promise, there is always that space of time that exists between God speaking the promise to us and the time when that promise becomes a reality. Sometimes that span of time is a moment, and sometimes it can be a lifetime. When

we have prayed all that God has asked us to pray, what do we do next? How do we live in the "until times" of life when the answers to our prayers are still in process?

THE UNTIL TIMES

The Book of Joshua is a great book about courage and conquest that always speaks to me. In chapter 8, Joshua and the nation of Israel were about to conquer the city of Ai. Their first attempt ended in failure because of the greed of one man. This was their second attempt, and they wanted to get it right.

The battle raged. In verse 26, we see that "Joshua kept holding out his spear until everyone who had lived in Ai was completely destroyed." Something struck me about the word "until." The battle continued successfully as long as Joshua held out his spear, *until everyone who lived in Ai was completely destroyed.* Those are heavy words. People were being slaughtered. An entire city was being decimated.

Had Joshua not held out his spear, there would have been no victory for Israel. Simply holding out a spear in Joshua's day (or having a modern-day commander point his pistol in the direction of the

battle) is dramatic-looking, but it's really only a gesture.

Something more than a gesture was taking place as Joshua stood with this spear raised. Miracles occur from the postures God has us assume in the "until time" seasons of life. In each "until time," there is an assignment for those who are waiting. Our cooperation with God links us with His planned victory. Prayer is our posture of faith in the "until times."

I did a search on the word "until" in the Scriptures and discovered that it is used hundreds of times—483 times to be exact. The word "until" was used in conjunction with winning battles, believing for God's promises, staying on track in ministry, and simply living life. Here are several of those occurrences to help illustrate what happens in these "until times":

➢ Genesis 8: The dove Noah released to search for dry land flew back and forth *until* the floodwaters on the earth had evaporated. This "until time" required the earth to get ready to receive the survivors of the flood. Noah, his family, and the animals all wanted to get out of the Ark, but it was still too early. "Until times" teach

us the value of waiting on God. His timing will always provide us with a place to live and survive. A muddy world is a premature world that can bog us down and get us killed if we launch out too early. Our prayers and declarations from the throne of God carry His timing, not ours. Patience in the wait reveals whether we truly are trusting God.

➤ Exodus 17: Aaron and Hur held up Moses' arms *until* the Amalekites were defeated. Arms down and they would lose. Arms up and they would win. With assistance, Moses' arms stayed up, and the Israelites won the battle. In battles we need help. In the "until times," we learn the value of faithful friends who stick with us in the fight and hold our arms up. These are the people who are there to celebrate the victory with us because they remained faithful to us in the battle.

➤ Exodus 33: Moses was hid in the cleft of the rock; the Lord covered Moses with His hand *until* the presence of God passed him by. The hand of God covered the man of

God so that he could survive the glory of God. In these experiences we learn to stay in the places of spiritual safety God has assigned for us.

> Numbers 32: An entire generation wandered in the wilderness *until* the unbelieving ones died off. It took forty years. Unbelief had to die off for the promise to be seen. Unbelief only sees giants. Belief sees God standing over giants. In the wilderness wanderings, attitudes had to be checked daily to make sure they aligned with the promise. In this "until time," God's people learned that the smallest element of unbelief has to be confronted early, or it will lead to death and wandering.

> Joshua 3: The priests stepped out over the waters of the Jordan River at flood stage, and the waters parted when their feet touched the foaming torrent. God stacked up the water, and the ground became dry, remaining dry *until* all the people passed through. It must have been nerve wracking to look up at a wall of water suspended in

an other-worldly form. A reality surfaced that day; if the Israelites wanted to get to the promise they would have to trust God to hold back the flood *until* they crossed over. They learned a new level of trust in the "until time."

> Joshua 6: During the Battle of Jericho, the children of Israel were told to remain silent *until* the seventh day. Then they were told to yell with all their might. At the yell the walls of the city fell down. When you seem to have the upper hand in a battle as Israel did that day—they vastly outnumbered the inhabitants of Jericho—it is easy to rush the process with human confidence and move ahead in your own strength instead of waiting for the miracle. The more it seems we can do things in our own strength, the easier it is to yell on day three instead of waiting for day seven. This "until time" in the battle taught the Israelites patience to trust God's plan.

> Joshua 10: The Lord caused the sun to stand still, and He extended the day *until* the nation of Israel defeated its enemies in a

prolonged battle. God asked Israel to continue fighting into times of day normally used for eating and sleeping. This "until time" was an unusual day that God provided in which all the rules and time frames were altered. In this "until time," the people knew that they had one chance at obedience, and so they stayed in the fight *until* it was finished.

> I Kings 17: A starving widow was told by the prophet Elijah to use the last of her food to cook him a meal. Because of her obedience, she was told that she would have a miraculous provision of oil and flour in her containers *until* the famine ended. The "until time" for this widow involved waking up each day, walking over to containers that had been empty the night before, and expecting that they would be full.

> John 2: During the wedding feast at Cana, one of the guests complimented Jesus for saving the best wine *until* the last—wine made miraculously from water. This "until time" of waiting to serve the miracle wine

taught the disciples that God does better things later in the program when our natural resources have all run out. The disciples learned to live in the expectation that the best was yet to come.

> John 8: Jesus talked to a woman caught in the act of adultery who was dragged into His presence by a group of men who wanted to kill her for her sin. When Jesus asked her accusers to throw the first stone, they began to leave, one by one, *until* only Jesus was left with her. Her "until time" brought her face to face with what a real man should be, not the one she was sleeping with or the ones who felt assigned to destroy her. Her "until time" was a place of revelation where she learned how to honor herself as a woman.

> Acts 1: Jesus told His disciples not to leave Jerusalem *until* the Father had sent the gift of the Spirit. The Spirit's power was required for the disciples to be God's witness to the world. The Church had assignments that would require supernatural power. This empowering by God

would heal the sick and raise the dead. It would require the disciples to live each day in a dependence upon the presence and power of God to bring the Kingdom of heaven to earth.

> I Corinthians 11: Paul reminded the church that every time they ate the bread and drank the cup they would be announcing the Lord's death *until* His return. Each time the Church receives communion, we remember that Someone died so that many could live. These "until times" of remembrance help us learn to not fear death because Jesus has conquered its power.

> I Timothy 4: Paul instructed the young pastor to focus on reading the Scriptures, encouraging believers, and continuing to teach the Word *until* Paul made a return visit. At times, ministry can be a grind. You might wonder what you are supposed to do in the "until times." *Until* the church gets a certain size. *Until* so-and-so hears God. *Until* a new season unfolds. *Until* a certain healing is experienced. Paul told Timothy

to stick with the basics of his calling, and the rest of it would all work out.

> II Timothy 1: Paul wrote a second letter to this same struggling shepherd. Paul shared his confidence in God to guard what he had entrusted to Timothy *until* the day of His return. Paul was trying to jump-start the fire in this young pastor's calling. In this "until time," Timothy learned that God keeps things of value secure in His hands. Anything in Timothy's hands would become fragile and insecure. This "until time" for Timothy meant learning to live in the grip of God and not in the grip of personal fear.

> I Peter 1: Peter told a persecuted church that God was protecting them by His power *until* they received their salvation which would be revealed on the last day. They painfully and sacrificially learned that the fear of martyrdom would come to them in their "until times," but when the temporary pain was past, the reward of eternity would embrace them forever.

These people who lived in the "until times" were not superheroes. They were people just like us who were interacting with God in faith. The most profound thing many of them did was to simply obey and continue obeying the last thing God said to them until the "until time" brought them to the promise.

My pastor and mentor, Roy Hicks, Jr., once shared a key to blessing with a group of us who were pastors in training. Roy said, "Just show up." Just show up in your marriage, and be faithful to your spouse and your children. Just show up at your place of employment, and do the best you can. Just show up when your friends need you, and cover them in their time of need. Simply showing up where we are expected to be keeps us in position for the coming miracles of God. Just showing up where God has called us can be the answer to someone's prayer. God wants us present when He pours out His Spirit.

These "until times" will accompany the life of one who prays from the throne of God. When we pray this way, we are speaking from eternity into time. Once the word of the Lord is spoken, developing time must yield to His word. God wants us to cultivate a life free from an impatience in prayer; He wants us to understand the purpose of

the "until times." He wants us to live in active expectation as we wait for the answers to our prayers.

15

EXPECTATION IN PRAYER

Jim Stephens, a good friend of mine, is now in his late sixties. He grew up working on his family ranch and was then called by God to walk away from that life and enter the ministry. He has been all over the world training leaders, planting churches, and starting training institutes. He has served God faithfully but has few of the physical possessions our culture equates with success.

Jim wrote something on his blog recently that really touched me:

> Sometimes I think, "What would life have been like if I had spent the same years building a business as I did being a missionary and pastor? Where would I be, and what would I have to show for my work at this stage in my life?" So much of what I have now is very intangible. And here's the scary thing

about it—if I stop believing, I have nothing. The only way to have a sense of satisfaction and achievement about how I've spent the years of my life, is to believe—to believe that Jesus is real, that God called me to do what I have done, and eternity is what really matters.

I was struck by the phrase, "if I stop believing, I have nothing." I asked myself: where in my life am I living like this? Where is the raw belief and expectation that causes me to be truly dependent upon God? This isn't about where we live on the economic scale but where we stand in our belief. A rich man can say this, and a poor man can say this. This believing posture is that place of faith where we choose to make God our only option.

When the Azusa Street Revival was taking place, expectation was high. The people on Azusa Street were in the same place my friend found himself. They knew that unless God showed up nothing was going to happen. All they could do was believe. The saints on Azusa Street expected God to move when they gathered, and He did. They expected the blind to see, the lame to walk, limbs to grow out, and the deaf to hear. And these things happened. Expectation changes the spiritual environment of our lives.

In 1906 people would travel to Los Angeles

from all over the world for business and pleasure. Many would arrive by train. Historical records tell us that the glory of God flowed out from the meeting place on Azusa Street into the surrounding neighborhoods. People exiting a train would step off onto the arrival platform and fall down under the power of God. They had no idea that just a short distance away one of the greatest revivals in modern history was taking place. The glory of God was flooding the city.

One young Hispanic boy lived near Azusa Street. Each day, he would look toward the building where the revival was happening. He knew the meetings had started when he saw flames of fire appear on the roof. These were not the flames of a natural fire but of God's Spirit.

Los Angeles was experiencing the glory of God because the Church was living in the expectation that God was at work in their midst. The hope of a city is the Church living in expectation of God. Real hope for our cities is not found in a newly elected government official, a unique community program, or a well-crafted budget. The hope of a city is the Church rising in her calling and aligning herself with the will of God.

In the Book of Matthew, Jesus instructed His disciples to go out and preach the Kingdom by

healing the sick, cleansing lepers, raising the dead, and casting out demons. He told His disciples that this kind of ministry would bring them persecution. He told them to fear God, not man. He told them to take up their cross and follow Him:

> When Jesus had finished giving these instructions to his twelve disciples, he went off teaching and preaching in towns throughout the country. John the Baptist, who was now in prison, heard about all the things the Messiah was doing. So he sent his disciples to ask Jesus, "Are you really the Messiah we've been waiting for, or should we keep looking for someone else?" Jesus told them, "Go back to John and tell him about what you have heard and seen—the blind see, the lame walk, the lepers are cured, the deaf hear, the dead are raised to life, and the Good News is being preached to the poor. And tell him: 'God blesses those who are not offended by me.'"
>
> —Matthew 11:1-6

John the Baptist was in prison awaiting his execution. In just a few days, his decapitated head would be presented as a macabre party favor to a dancer in the king's court. John found himself wondering whether Jesus was the real thing. This is the same John who was there at the beginning of the Lord's ministry when the skies opened up, the Spirit descended upon Jesus, and the very voice of God

spoke from heaven. John saw the miraculous affirmation of Jesus but later found himself wondering. Places of imprisonment can do this to a person. The past miracles are not what comfort us in places like this. We need a real-time word from the Lord.

The answer that Jesus sent back, "the blind see, the lame walk, the lepers are cured, the deaf hear, the dead are raised to life, and the Good News is being preached to the poor" is an answer with evidence. The evidence is what John needed to hear to confirm that Jesus was the Messiah.

We need to live in the expectation of evidence from God:

> ## WE CAN EXPECT THAT GOD WILL BE WITH US

"No, I will not abandon you as orphans—I will come to you."

—John 14:18

No matter where we find ourselves, Jesus promises to come to us with the evidence of His love and presence, affirming us as His children.

> ## WE CAN EXPECT TO BE EMPOWERED BY GOD

But when the Holy Spirit has come upon you, you will receive power and will tell people about me everywhere—in Jerusalem, throughout Judea, in Samaria, and to the ends of the earth.

—Acts 1:8

God promised to send His power to us. What God calls us to accomplish in His name cannot be done in human strength or strategy. God is faithful; we can expect His supernatural power to be there when we need it because He made a promise that we would receive the power.

> ## WE CAN EXPECT TO DO THE GREATER WORKS OF JESUS CHRIST

"The truth is, anyone who believes in me will do the same works I have done, and even greater works, because I am going to be with the Father."

—John 14:12

The greater works come because Jesus has sent the Spirit back to the Church:

Now he sits on the throne of highest honor in heaven, at God's right hand. And the Father, as he had promised, gave him the Holy Spirit to pour out upon us, just as you see and hear today.

—Acts 2:33

The Lord sits above all power structures, world governments, diseases, and demonic powers. We as the Church are now seated with Him in the heavenly realms. We live in two realms: here on earth and with Him in eternity. As Jesus pours the Spirit upon the Church on earth, the descending flow of God's presence carries with it the power to break the chains that imprison people.

> ## ➤ WE CAN EXPECT THAT JESUS WILL PROVE HIMSELF TRUE

During the forty days after his crucifixion, he appeared to the apostles from time to time and proved to them in many ways that he was actually alive. On these occasions he talked to them about the Kingdom of God.

—Acts 1:3

Jesus comes to His Church and to the unbelieving world to prove He is alive. His proof is found in the answer Jesus sent back to John the Baptist. This proof is what Peter said in Acts 2:33 when he spoke to the crowd on the Day of Pentecost, "just as you see and hear today." When God

shows up, what He does will be seen and heard. God doesn't show up as a voiceless theory or an invisible concept. He makes His presence known by bringing the evidence of heaven down upon the earth.

When we expect God to come, that expectant mindset will change everything. No longer is our life a holding pattern for heaven. We begin to believe now, in this present hour, the message Jesus sent back to John in prison. That message helped John refocus on the Lord and then die in peace.

16

EXTENDING AN INVITATION

> Then as I looked, I saw a door standing open in
> heaven, and the same voice I had heard before spoke
> to me with the sound of a mighty trumpet blast. The
> voice said, "Come up here, and I will show you
> what must happen after these things."
>
> —Revelation 4:1-2

Around the throne of God is the beauty of precious
gemstones, flashes of lighting and thunder, displays
of light, and worship that focuses on the One Who
sits upon the throne. The throne of God is a
powerful place to be and to experience.

In my fiftieth year, I was asked by a friend if I
would like to climb to the top of Mount
McLoughlin. This mountain is over 9,000 feet high
and is the prominent landmark in our area of
Southern Oregon. Throughout a good portion of the

year, it is snow capped. During the late summer the snow is gone, and many people climb to the summit.

I like to hike, but I am no mountain climber. Thankfully, Mount McLoughlin can be hiked by most people in average physical condition. We left early in the morning and drove to the trailhead. On the way up, it seemed that the summit kept getting farther away. Finally, we made it.

The view from 9,000 feet put the entire region in perspective. Like hundreds before me, I looked out on the surrounding area. I could see the Klamath Lakes, Mount Shasta to the south, and the Rogue Valley before me. As I strained to look over the valley, I could make out the vicinity where our church was located. I had an idea.

I reached into my backpack, pulled out my cell phone, and tried to get a signal. Amazingly, the phone showed a strong signal. I called the church office many miles away and said "hello" from 9,000 feet above the valley floor. I wanted the church staff to know their pastor was looking down upon them from thousands of feet above.

On top of that mountain, I knew that the daily business of life was taking place below me. But here I was high above it all. This is similar to viewing prayer from the throne of God. We call in from a

place above the daily turmoil and release a perspective that is only possible from higher elevations.

As we come to the end of this book on prayer from the throne of God, I would like to invite you "to come up here." Come up and begin to realize where you are seated in Christ. While John's invitation to come up is something yet to happen in the future, this invitation to come up and add heaven as another prayer altar is available for the Church today.

I invite you today to pray for your family from the throne of God. See your spouse and your children from His perspective. Declare, decree, and prophesy hope to your loved ones. I invite you to come up to the throne of God and pray over His Church in your city from this exalted position and to declare God's heart over His people and over your place of service. Declare provision for the impoverished. Decree justice to your nation. I invite you to come up and see the world from the Redeemer's perspective and to prophesy His hope back upon the earth and believe that He has plans to revive our world.

Coming up to a higher place changes everything we see and will eventually change everything we pray. God put us next to Him in

Christ for a purpose greater than just seeing the commanding view. He placed us there to command the things of this life to come into line with the destiny and heart God has for our world.